LBJ

# LBJ

## THE WHITE HOUSE YEARS

# LBJ

## THE WHITE HOUSE YEARS

### HARRY MIDDLETON

HARRY N. ABRAMS, INC., PUBLISHERS, NEW YORK

Editor: MARK D. GREENBERG
Designer: LLOYD ZIFF

Library of Congress Cataloging-in-Publication Data
Middleton, Harry J. (Harry Joseph), 1921–
LBJ: the White House years / by Harry Middleton.
p.  cm.
Includes bibliographical references.
ISBN 0–8109–1191–4
1. Johnson, Lyndon B. (Lyndon Baines), 1908–1973—Pictorial works.
2. United States—Politics and government—1963–1969—Pictorial works.
3. United States—Politics and government—1963–1969.
I. Title.

E847.M52  1990          89–39938          973.923'092—dc20
                        CIP

The Publisher thanks the following people
for having given their permission to cite them in this book:
(original contributions)
Bess Abell, Liz Carpenter, Luci Baines Johnson, Tom Johnson, Mathilde and Arthur Krim,
Charles S. Robb, Lynda Johnson Robb, Theodore C. Sorensen;
(from oral histories on deposit at the LBJ Library)
[Mrs.] Wilbur Cohen, Mrs. Lyndon B. Johnson, Harry C. McPherson, Jr.;
(from remarks delivered at the LBJ Library)
Joseph A. Califano, Carol Channing, Clark M. Clifford,
Barbara C. Jordan, Bill D. Moyers, Walt Rostow;
(from films on deposit at the LBJ Library)
Horace Busby, Douglass Cater, Marie Fehmer Chiarodo;
(from previously published material)
Jacqueline Kennedy Onassis [from *The Way We Were: 1963, The Year Kennedy Was Shot,*
edited by Robert MacNeil, published by Carroll & Graf, New York, 1988];
George Reedy [from *Lyndon B. Johnson: A Memoir,*
published by Andrews and McMeel, Inc., New York, 1982];
and Jack Valenti [from *A Very Human President,*
published by W.W. Norton & Co., Inc., New York, 1975]

# CONTENTS

Yoichi Okamoto, a first-generation American,

was a photographer for the United States Information Agency in 1963,

when he was assigned to cover the new President of the United States.

He might have seen this assignment as ceremonial,

an opportunity to enhance the public relations of his boss.

But he did not. What he did instead, as a photojournalist, was show

how a Presidency can be captured on film and documented for history.

He is responsible for most of the photographs in this book,

which is dedicated to his memory.

# PREFACE

**T**his book is a pictorial reflection of President Lyndon Johnson's activities—those that the White House photographers were able to cover. It is not a history of the 1960s, nor is it a comprehensive account of Johnson's Presidency. So, to that extent, it is a decidedly limited report.

But within those strictures, it is unique. Johnson was the first Chief Executive to give White House photographers virtually unlimited access to him and his daily routine. With that passport into public times and private ones, the gifted Yoichi Okamoto and his enterprising team pioneered in compiling a pictorial record of a Presidency. Frank Wolfe, a member of that team, carried the assignment into the President's retirement, and his work is represented chiefly in the Epilogue.

The text accompanying the photographs is an account of Johnson's White House years and his retirement, based largely on the historical record available to everyone. I have listed in the Bibliography the books and other documents I consulted, but the source of some information is my own experience and memory. After working for President Johnson in the White House, I came with him to Texas—first, along with other former Administration aides, to help him compile his memoirs; then, to take over the directorship of the library housing his papers. Wherever I found it appropriate, in the course of writing this book, I have drawn freely on that experience.

I took leave from my job to work on this project. Before I return to that job, I would like, as a researcher, to thank the incomparable staff of the LBJ Library for the assistance I have been given. I single out Philip Scott, Regina Greenwell, Robert Tissing, and Frank Wolfe because of their individual contributions. But I know, as perhaps not all researchers do, that in one way or another the entire staff supports each request for assistance.

I extend my thanks also to Dorothy Olding, who steered this book in the right direction, and to Paul Gottlieb, who as publisher brought the book into being and supported it unstintingly. Mark Greenberg was patient, encouraging, clear-eyed, and helpful—all those things a writer hopes an editor will be —but more: from the beginning of the project he had a wonderful feeling for it, a road map in his mind from which the book took its organization and clarity. The designer, Lloyd Ziff, is a wonder. In his sensitive hands the photographs were given the life they deserve.

Finally, I am grateful to those whose reminiscences of the 36th President of the United States have infused this book with a special flavor and color.

—HARRY MIDDLETON
New York City, September 1989

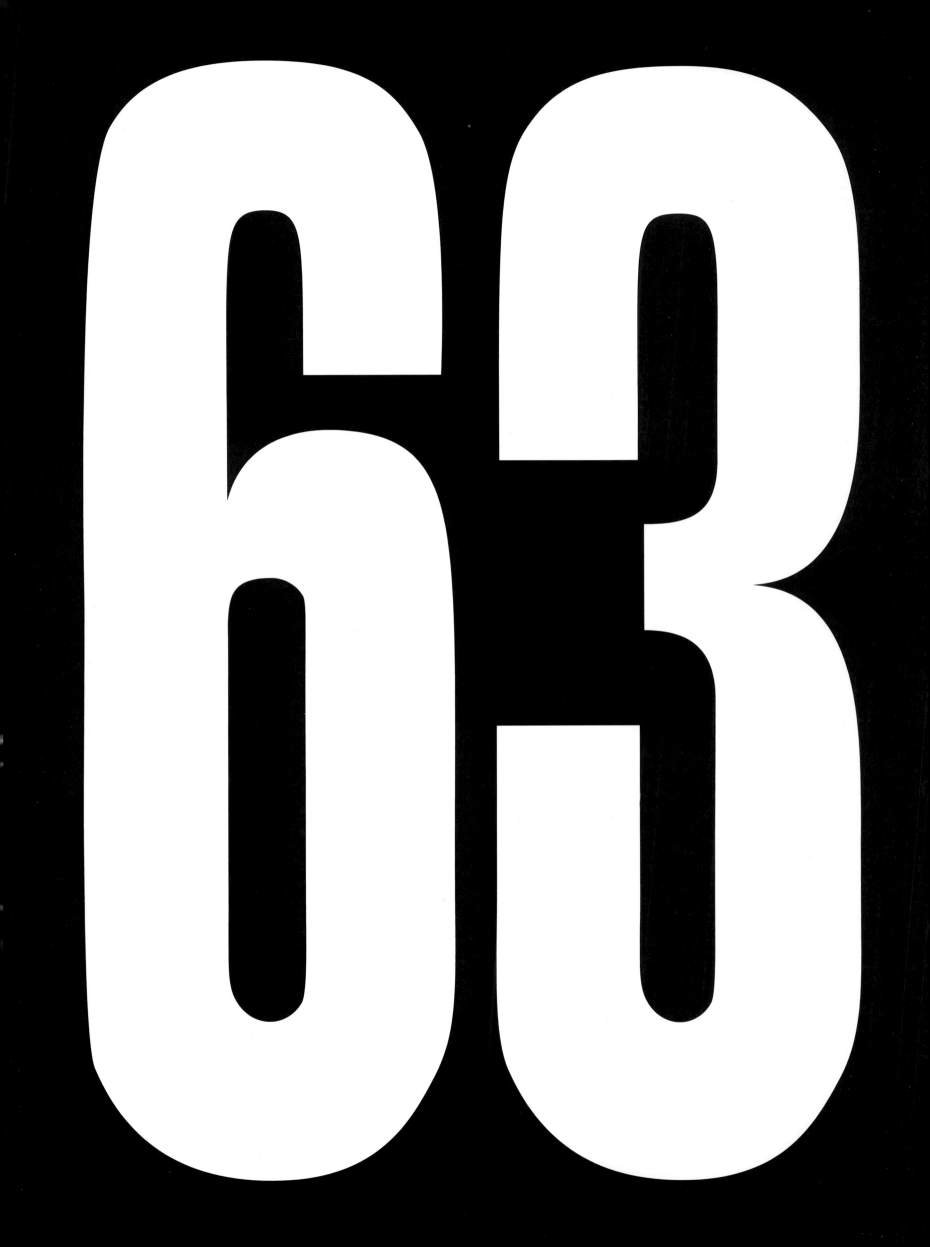

*Lyndon Johnson was extraordinary; he did everything he could to be magnanimous, to be kind. It must have been very difficult for him. I don't know exactly how long [it was] before I could move. I moved out of the White House as quickly as I could, but it was a period of about [ten days or so]…Now that I look back on it, I think I should have gotten out the next —I didn't have any place to go…*

*I suppose one was in a state of shock, packing up. But President Johnson made you feel that you and your children [could stay], a great courtesy to a woman in distress.*

*It's funny what you do in a state of shock. I remember going over to the Oval Office to ask him for two things. They were two things I thought I would like to ask him as a favor.*

*One was to name the space center in Florida "Cape Kennedy." Now that I think back on it, that was so wrong, and if I'd known [Cape Canaveral] was the name from the time of Columbus, it would be the last thing that Jack would have wanted. The reason I asked was, I can remember this first speech Jack made in Texas was that there would be a rocket one day that would go to the moon. I kept thinking, "That's going to be forgotten, and his dreams are going to be forgotten." I had this terrible fear then that he'd be forgotten, and I thought, "Well, maybe they'll remember someday that this man did dream that…"*

*And the other one, which is so trivial, was: there were plans for the renovation of Washington, and there was this commission, and I thought it might come to an end. I asked President Johnson if he'd be nice enough to receive the commission and sort of give approval to the work they were doing, and he did. It was one of the first things he did…*

*I almost felt sorry for [President Johnson], because I knew he felt sorry for me. There wasn't anything anyone could do about it, but I think the situation gave him pain, and he tried to do the best he could. And he did, and I was really touched by that generosity of spirit…I always felt that about him…*

—JACQUELINE KENNEDY ONASSIS

from: *The Way We Were: 1963, The Year Kennedy Was Shot.*
Robert MacNeil, editor;
New York: Carroll & Graf, 1988

Members of the Kennedy family lead his funeral procession from the White House.

T he Lyndon Johnson who bestrode the years of his presidency like a colossus was virtually unknown to the American people when they first saw him as their leader. He had been a dominant force in the 1950s when he was making a record as the most effective Senate majority leader of the 20th century. But that was a smaller stage; his performance had been observed only by official Washington, hardly at all by the rest of the country. As Vice President under John Kennedy, he had been lost to general view. So when a numbed and grieving nation looked to its new leader in the nightmare hours following Kennedy's assassination on a Dallas street on November 22, 1963, it saw a stranger.

But through the fog of anguish and apprehension, that stranger took form first as a solicitous figure sensitive to the tragedy that suffused the country, attentive to its need for reassurance, and then as a forceful leader moving confidently to assure the continuity of government.

It seemed in those early days that he knew instinctively what to do. "He came to the office," said Douglass Cater, who covered him as a writer for *Reporter* magazine and soon joined his White House staff, "with an encyclopedic knowledge of everything that had happened in Washington since he first arrived there thirty years before." He touched all the power buttons, conferring with former Presidents and foreign dignitaries; with leaders in Congress, labor, industry, and civil rights; with the governors of all 50 states; with key mayors and trusted advisers and with the Cabinet he inherited, beseeching them to stay with him and provide a smooth transference of Presidential power.

He appointed a blue-ribbon commission to investigate the circumstances of President Kennedy's murder, and he persuaded the reluctant Chief Justice of the United States, Earl Warren, to serve as chairman. The commission's finding, that a lone psychotic gunman was the sole assassin, would eventually draw skeptics (including Johnson himself), but at the time, establishing the commission was another heartening bit of evidence that even in tragedy the country could handle its problems.

He even assumed the role of the nation's chief labor negotiator to prevent a nationwide railroad strike.

It was all a masterful exercise in statecraft. "History will record," said *Time* correspondent Hugh Sidey, "the great contribution Lyndon Johnson made in taking us through the transition. The one man who knew more about government than anyone else was there, and he became President."

He sought to assure the continuity not only of the nation's system of government but also of the programs and policies of the fallen leader. In an appearance

(previous pages)

**Flanked by his wife and a stricken Jacqueline Kennedy, Lyndon Baines Johnson takes the Oath of Office as President of the United States aboard Air Force One after the assassination of President Kennedy in Dallas.**

**H**e was many things:

*proud, sensitive, impulsive, flamboyant, sentimental, earthy, mean at times, bold,*

*euphoric, insecure, magnanimous, the best dancer in the White House since Washington,*

*but temperamental, melancholy, and strangely ill at ease as well. He had an animal sense*

*of weakness in other men, on whom he could inflict a hundred cuts.*

*But character is something that Presidents transcend. And those of us who worked for*

*him were willing to forgive his personal flaws, as he forgave ours, because in his best*

*moments he had such a large and generous vision of America as a prosperous, caring,*

*just society.*

—BILL MOYERS

before a joint session of Congress five days after Dallas, he echoed Kennedy's memorable inaugural call, "Let us begin," with the summons: "Let us continue."

The Congress, dominated by conservatives, had brought Kennedy's more liberal legislative program to a standstill. It had spurned his pleas for Federal aid to education and medical insurance for the elderly, and his other proposals were holed up in uncooperative committees. Johnson saw his task as getting them unstuck, sent to the floor, and passed.

To those bills already stalled in the legislative hopper, he added another. Learning in the early hours of his Presidency that the Council of Economic Advisers had, with Kennedy's approval, been conducting research for a plan to combat poverty, he gave instructions to proceed with it at top speed; and six weeks later, in his State of the Union Address, he dramatically declared war on poverty. A team assembled by Sargent Shriver, head of the Peace Corps, labored through the nights so a program could go to Congress with provisions to give a "head start" to deprived youngsters starting school, and job training to unskilled men and women, and in a dozen other ways tackle the conditions that trap people in a cycle of poverty.

Johnson played the Kennedy card tirelessly. In every forum open to him, sensing what he described as "a genuine desire for unity on the part of most people," the new President exploited the national mood of grief and urged enactment of his martyred predecessor's programs. He set to the task with

**The President reviews a speech draft in the front hall of the Executive Mansion with Jack Valenti, a new member of his staff.**

(previous page)
**The new President, now occupying the Oval Office, confronts one of the first crises of his Administration, the dispute in Panama.**

what seemed to be superhuman energy and the skills honed in his years on Capitol Hill. "If any sense were to come of the senseless events which had brought me to the...Presidency," he wrote later, "it would come only from my using the experience I had gained as a legislator."

That experience was consensus building, vote getting, and vote counting. He considered politics to be "the art of the possible," but that was no simple exercise in pragmatism. For Johnson, Douglass Cater said, seeking a consensus "was trying to find the maximum you could get a majority to support." Johnson himself defined that maximum as "the greatest good for the greatest number." The currency for achieving it was votes, and he was a master at marshaling them. Those who had watched him in action in the Senate vividly attested to his attention to detail, his considerable presence and personality, his intimate knowledge of those who had the votes. Said William S. White, who covered him for the New York *Times* through his Senate years: "He was constantly on the floor, keeping in touch with the interests, the desires, the weaknesses of the other fellow. His method of persuasion was legendary—cajoling, wheedling, scaring. He didn't actually blackmail anybody, but he would throw in a fairly stiff reminder that you might want this bill or something else next week..." Bill Moyers, who had started working for him as a young man, observed: "He knew how to reach you...Sometimes it could be a judgeship for a friend's nephew. Sometimes it could be the hint of a threat. Sometimes it could be playing to your dream of immortality. Sometimes it was just stroking your conscience." "Johnson got votes," said Hubert Humphrey, who had headed the Senate's liberal forces during Johnson's leadership, "by whispering in ears and pulling lapels and standing nose to nose." "He said the only power he had was the power to persuade," recalled Ralph Huitt, a Senate committee assistant. "God Almighty, that's like saying the only wind we have is a hurricane."

He would not move on a piece of legislation until he was sure he had the votes in hand, and then he acted swiftly, often calling an item to the floor before the opposition had time to rally.

Those were skills he carried into the White House and used extensively. "Faced with the choice of being President or Senate majority leader," said Robert Hardesty, who became a White House aide, "he chose both."

The Presidency's "bully pulpit," as Theodore Roosevelt called it, has considerable powers of its own, and Johnson took advantage of them as well. To dramatize the existence of the poor—who had been generally hidden from public view until a few pivotal studies and books revealed their presence—he

visited families scratching out a bare survival in the hollows of Appalachia, making sure that the conditions in which they lived were recorded by the reporters and photographers trailing him, and revealed to the nation.

With his words and his actions, the new President was defining a progressive position for himself, which came as a surprise to many—although, as he later observed, "it shouldn't have, if they really knew me." He had started his government career as a New Deal Congressman in 1937, when he was 29 years old, loyally supporting the programs of Franklin Roosevelt. His central Texas hill country constituents, rejoicing in the electrification he and the New Deal had brought them, permitted—even applauded—it. As Senator, he had responded to a broader state constituency, which included some decidedly conservative interests. ("You can't do anyone any good if you can't be elected," he said.) He was recognized as a generally moderate Senator, and he forged an effective working relationship with the Senate's liberal leaders, but he was never mistaken for a liberal himself in those years.

Now he was stumping the country on behalf of people who had never had a stake in society or a voice in government. When Cater asked why he was taking on what appeared to be the hopeless cause of poverty, which had no powerful constituents, he answered as the populist the early Lyndon Johnson had been: "I don't know if we will pass a single program or appropriate a single dollar. But before I'm through, no community in America is going to be able to ignore the poverty in its midst." Speaking to a group of newspaper editors, he declared: "People are just not going to stand and see their children starve and be driven out of school and be eaten up with disease in the twentieth century... They will forgo [violence] as long as they can, but they are going to eat, and they are going to learn, and they are going to grow." (Later, in retirement, he reflected on the same theme, even more vividly: "If men have to watch their families starve and die, there will be a revolution in this country, and it won't necessarily be benign.")

It was with his concern for the plight of black Americans that he made his most decisive stand. Moyers, who became Johnson's chief lieutenant for shepherding domestic programs, later recalled: "There grew in his mind—you could see it taking shape—the decision to make equal justice and equal opportunity the first and primary theater of action for his Administration." In his first appeal to Congress, the new President challenged that body to memorialize Kennedy with passage of the slain President's stalled civil rights bill, and he coupled that challenge with his own moral summons. "We have talked long

**The President meets with his full Cabinet soon after taking office.**

enough in this country about equal rights," he said. "We have talked for a hundred years or more. It is time now to write the next chapter, and to write it in the books of law."

Johnson had personally deplored the convention of segregation and white supremacy that prevailed in the South. "Lyndon Johnson hated Jim Crow," Moyers said. "He despised this vicious tar baby to which his South had been for so long stuck, and he wanted, the first chance he could, to dispatch the tar baby to the past." As Vice President, he had spoken forcefully and eloquently for converting Lincoln's Emancipation from a "proclamation" into a "fact," and as the head of a Presidentially appointed commission, he had helped to open a number of business and labor doors to blacks. As Senate majority leader, he had

masterminded a civil rights law in 1957—weakened through compromise, but nonetheless the first to pass the Congress in almost a century. As Senator, he had refused to sign a Southern manifesto criticizing the Supreme Court's historic declaration that segregation in public schools was unconstitutional.

For all that, however, it remained that he had voted against several proposed civil rights bills.

And now he was putting the power and prestige of the Presidency behind sweeping legislation that would outlaw discrimination in restaurants, hotels, and other accommodations—and in the process, he was even abandoning the techniques of compromise with which he had earned his reputation. He refused to consider any modification of the bill whatever, and through the

**In his first days in office, LBJ touches all the power buttons. Here, the President confers with a key Senator, Russell Long of Louisiana.**

(above) **Johnson with union leaders George Meany and Andrew Biemiller;** (left) **civil rights leaders Martin Luther King, Whitney Young, and James Farmer;** (right) **liberal Congressman Emanuel Cellar and** (far right) **conservative Senator Barry Goldwater.**

**H**e was a complex, contradictory personality. I have heard him, when we were on his ranch going by and watching the animals, refer to all sorts of sexual characteristics of the animals and of people, and then five minutes later you could stand on the hillside there watching the sunset and you'd find a man who was a poet describing the sunset and the relationship of the land to the people and his hopes and aspirations for people. And it seems to me that people who talk about his crudity do not understand that this was an earthy man...a combination of Boccaccio and Machiavelli and John Keats.      —WILBUR COHEN

**H**e was an awesome engine of a man: terrorizing; tender; inexhaustibly energetic; ruthless; loving of land, grass, and water; engulfing; patient; impatient; caring; insightful; devoted to wife, family, and friends; petty; clairvoyant; compassionate; bullying; sensitive; tough; resolute; charming; earthy; courageous; devious; full of humor; brilliantly

**A**s a human being he was a miserable person...a bully, sadist, lout, and egotist...His lapses from civilized conduct were deliberate and usually intended to subordinate someone else to his will. He did disgusting things because he realized that other people had to pretend that they did not mind. It was his method of bending them to his designs.

Were there nothing to look at save LBJ's personal relationships with other people, it would be merciful to forget him altogether. But there is much more to look at. He may have been a son of a bitch, but he was a colossal son of a bitch...Nevertheless, he was capable of inspiring strong attachments even with people who knew him for what he was.

—GEORGE REEDY
from: *Lyndon B. Johnson: A Memoir*
New York: Andrews and McMeel, 1982

intelligent; brutal; wise; suspicious; disciplined; crafty; generous . . . He had one goal: to be the greatest president doing the greatest good in the history of the nation. He had one tragedy: a war

whose commitments he could not break and whose tenacity he did not perceive.

—JACK VALENTI
from: *A Very Human President*
New York: W.W. Norton, 1975

spring, while the Senate was locked in the longest filibuster in its history, he held firm, prepared to sacrifice all other legislation to get this one through. The opposition was organized by Georgia's Richard Russell, his old friend and mentor who more than anyone else was responsible for Johnson, at age 44, becoming the youngest leader the Senate had ever had. Presidential aide Jack Valenti was present when the two men met one Sunday afternoon, and as he recalled it: "They talked as old friends talk. Then the President, with a mark of respect and deference, said to Senator Russell, 'Dick, we are going to have a civil rights bill. But there is going to be one big difference. We are not going to compromise, and I am going to fight you with everything I've got.' And Russell didn't answer, but he understood...After Johnson escorted Russell out, he came back and said to me, 'I love that man. It's going to hurt me to beat him. But if I don't beat him, this is all lost.'"

The battle on the Senate floor could be won only by getting two-thirds of the Senators to vote for cloture, the device that sets a time limit on debate, thus ending filibuster. That meant getting more Republicans on board than might normally be expected. To that end, Johnson and Hubert Humphrey—who was floor manager of the bill—worked tirelessly on Everett Dirksen, the florid and colorful—and conservative—minority leader. "We set out to make him a hero," Johnson said, and they did, convincing him that he would become celebrated if he helped carry the day for the bill. Dirksen dramatically revealed his recognition of equal justice as "an idea whose time has come," announced his support, and cloture followed.

When Johnson signed the bill in early June, his credentials as an activist President and a master of the Congress were secure. With him and his aides watching every vote, the legislative pipeline came unclogged, and a steady stream of new laws, including the poverty bill, came through—more than 400 in all.

Those victories were not even in place before he let it be known that others, even greater, would soon be on their way. He revealed his plans for a "Great Society" that would clear the agenda for social reform that had been awaiting action since Roosevelt's day. Federal aid to education and medical care for the elderly, although already rebuffed by Congress, would be resubmitted as top-priority items. After all that was accomplished, there would then begin the

T*his Administration, here and now, declares unconditional*

*war on poverty in America...It will not be a*

*short or easy struggle, no single weapon or*

*strategy will suffice, but we shall not rest*

*until that war is won...*

*Our aim is not only to relieve the symptoms*

*of poverty, but to cure it, and above all, to*

*prevent it.*

Annual Address to the Congress on the State of the Union
January 8, 1964

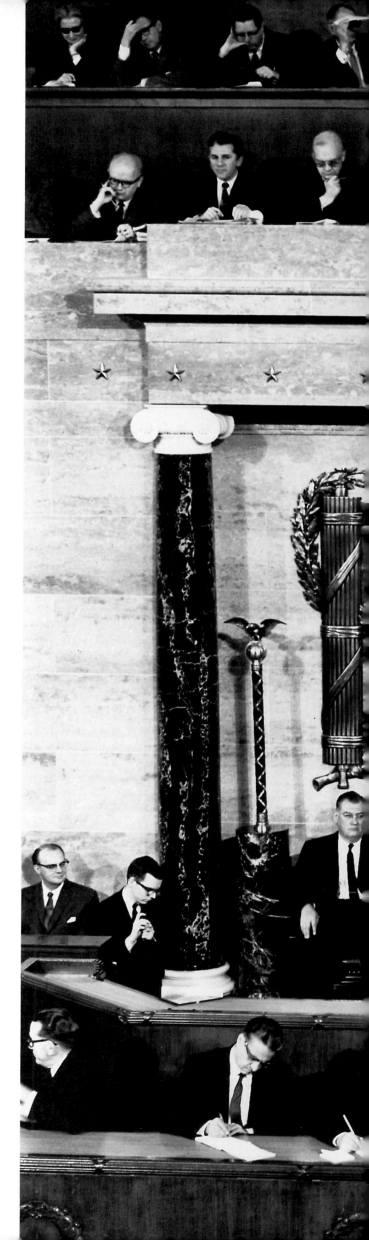

IN GOD WE TRUST

**A Presidential helicopter touching down is an unfamiliar sight in Appalachia as Johnson explores the conditions in which poor families in the region live. He gives Sargent Shriver, head of the Peace Corps, the additional job of directing the "war on poverty."**

"rebuilding of America," which would start with the saving of America. He saw in jeopardy not only the country's natural resources, its air and water, but just as important, its beauty. "Once our natural splendor is destroyed," he warned, "it can never be recaptured. And once man can no longer walk with beauty or wonder at nature his spirit will wither and his sustenance be wasted."

Programs to preserve beauty might be considered revolutionary, but then so well might the entire program. "Historians should make no mistake," Joseph A. Califano, Jr., said in an assessment some years later. "What Lyndon Johnson and the Great Society were about was revolution." (Califano was himself one of the architects of that revolution, having succeeded Moyers as LBJ's chief assistant for domestic programs.)

And with resources growing at the rate of 5 percent a year, Johnson's revolution would be driven by an economy that, in the words of his Council of Economic Advisers, would be "the mightiest engine of human progress the world has ever seen."

Whenever the President travels, there is extensive protection from the Secret Service, still reeling from the Kennedy assassination.

**H**e was many faceted, marvelous, contradictory, with a great natural intelligence, a showman, a man of unlimited hopes and beliefs in this country —but with, on the other hand, a little stream of leveling cynicism. His compassion was quite personal and genuine; it wasn't just philosophy from a book. He was full of faults, too, and sometimes misjudgments about people. But he was an awfully good man to have around in a tight spot.

I disagreed with him when he talked in times of anger; words out of your mouth have wings, and when

*they've flown off, you can't recall them. And they're remembered, and the hurts wind up by hurting the one who inflicted them. Lyndon was sometimes his own worst enemy. But he was also terribly sweet and caring and giving, and so much more generous than I was or most of the people I knew.*

*He was an exciting person to live with, and I consider myself very lucky. I know we were better together than we were apart.*

—LADY BIRD JOHNSON

Cheered on by Congressional leaders of both parties, LBJ throws out the first baseball of the 1964 season, and enjoys the popcorn. Not known particularly as a sports fan, he can nonetheless make political hay even at the stadium.

**F**or a century we labored to settle and to subdue a continent. For half a century we called upon

unbounded invention and untiring industry to create an order of plenty for all of our

people...In your time we have the opportunity to move not only toward the rich society and

the powerful society, but upward to the Great Society.

*The Great Society is not a safe harbor, a resting place, a final objective, a finished work. It is*

*a challenge constantly renewed, beckoning us toward a destiny where the meaning of our*

*lives matches the marvelous products of our labor.*

Commencement Address
University of Michigan
May 22, 1964

A stranger no longer, he now dominated the national scene. Courting Congressmen, swimming with clergymen, decorating a physicist who had been considered a security risk in the 1950s, swooping tourists up at the gate for a walk through the White House, leading reporters on a fast track around the grounds and chauffeuring them across the pastures of his ranch, standing his beagle on its hind legs by holding its ears—he was all over the front pages. The dignified restraint with which he had moved through the first, fearful days of uncertainty was still in evidence at times, but as the year wore on the country saw more and more of the exuberant and volatile Lyndon Johnson only a few had known before. The media reported his boundless energy, his overpowering presence, his talents on the dance floor, his attention to detail, his mastery of the legislative process, his instinct for power. More than one journal called him an "elemental force"; "larger than life" became a familiar phrase. The pundits probed his significance. "The shape of tomorrow's America," wrote historian-reporter Theodore H. White, "depends more on what goes on in his mind than in that of any individual since Lincoln."

But he was an atonal symphony of contradictions: he could be petty, crude, and cruel; he was a master of vulgarity—often a hilarious one—when it served his purpose. But he was also large-minded, magnanimous, compassionate, and capable of a wonderfully simple eloquence. A junior member of the Administration, encountering him for the first time in a White House meeting, reported to his boss: "He was power, embodied in a man—the kind of power that God could never have intended for a mortal man to wield. And yet he was talking about human things—about a ranch and about trees and rocks." No one could get him whole, and Theodore White summed up the frustration of those who tried: "He is so richly complicated a personality that...he defies ordinary political analysis."

From the start, Johnson wanted to seize the initiative in foreign affairs as he had on the domestic stage. He told his National Security Adviser, McGeorge Bundy, to get together a group of experts to develop some "peace initiatives" that would provide an alternative to having erupting crises "run me in the corner and me dodge like a Mexican bullfighter."

But it was not to be. Crises demanding action came soon. In early January, riots broke out in the Panama Canal Zone, which by treaty was under U.S. control, exacerbating a long-simmering tension over the terms of the then 60-year-old treaty. The Panamanians demanded renegotiation. Johnson refused to

**Johnson rejects Robert Kennedy as his Vice Presidential running mate in the 1964 election, but he campaigns vigorously for him when he runs for Senator from New York.**

An enthusiastic
Democratic
convention
in Atlantic City
nominates Johnson
and Senator Hubert
Humphrey, and
(following pages)
an ebullient LBJ
takes off on a
campaign trail
across America.

negotiate "at the point of a gun," but over a three-month period he engineered an accord that would enable the two countries to review the points of contention between them.

In the midst of all that, Fidel Castro cut off the water supply to the American naval base at Guantanamo Bay on Cuba's southeast coast, which the U.S. occupies by virtue of another treaty. This crisis was resolved by building a desalination plant and making the base independent of Cuban supplies of any kind.

And there was Vietnam.

It was to be Lyndon Johnson's nemesis, the dark beast he would wrestle for the rest of his time, which would grow to horrifying size and finally overpower him. But in those early days it did not seem so much a crisis as an important but nagging and long-standing problem.

From the perspective of a quarter-century later, burdened with awareness of the pain and confusion and anguish that the war in Vietnam brought to the American people, it is difficult to see it from the vastly different perspective of the time. But it *was* another day, with a perspective that seemed clear.

After a turbulent century of colonial occupation, war, and revolution, Vietnam had been divided in the 1950s into two states, a Communist regime led by Ho Chi Minh in the North, and the one in the South, under the presidency of Ngo Dinh Diem, generally pro-Western in its outlook. President Eisenhower had pledged assistance in the form of financial aid and military equipment to help the fledgling government of South Vietnam grow and defend itself. When Communist rebels in the South, the Viet Cong, supplied and eventually led by the North, began their insurgency in the early 1960s, President Kennedy increased U.S. assistance to include soldiers to advise and train South Vietnam's military forces. By the time of Kennedy's assassination there were 16,000 such advisers there, authorized to return fire if fired upon.

Despite dismaying signs of the instability of South Vietnam's government, it was generally believed that keeping the country free of Communist control was essential to American security. Less than three weeks before Kennedy's death, the situation was summed up this way:

> The American stake in South Vietnam is large. The country is vital to the whole Western defense position in Southeast Asia.
>
> South Vietnam holds the key to the Indo-Chinese peninsula and thus to the whole of Southeast Asia.
>
> Communist control of South Vietnam would almost surely mean the collapse of the shaky coalition regime in Laos; it would put enormous pressure on pro-Western Thailand and on the neutralist regimes in Cambodia and Burma. The lands to the south—Malaya and Indonesia—and the entire allied position in the western Pacific would be in severe jeopardy. India, already under pressure along its borders from Communist China, would be outflanked. Communist China's drive for hegemony would be enormously enhanced.
>
> Loss of South Vietnam to the Communists would raise doubts around the globe about the value of U.S. commitments to defend nations against Communist pressure.

That was not an isolated, warmongering voice. It was the editorial position of the influential New York *Times*, and the dangers it saw were very real to most of the American people in 1963.

They were real to Lyndon Johnson.

He believed, as fervently as his predecessor had, that the line must be held in Vietnam—and that the United States had an obligation as a member of the Southeast Asia Treaty Organization to help South Vietnam hold it. He believed, as devoutly as did the *Times* and most of the American people then, that to do otherwise would be to permit aggression to succeed, which would inevitably lead to Communist control of all of Southeast Asia, endangering our strategic

The President sees his wife off as she sets forth on a campaign swing through the South. Never before has a First Lady campaigned alone on behalf of her husband. From the platform of the LADY BIRD SPECIAL, Lady Bird Johnson defends the Administration's civil rights program, adroitly fends off hecklers, and declares that she wants to demonstrate that the South is "a beloved place to this President and his wife." She garners considerable goodwill.

position throughout the Pacific, and drastically increasing the chances of another world war. To him, as to most of the political leaders of his generation, the lessons from World War II were clear: to prevent war, you had to be willing to stop aggression, wherever and whenever it occurred. Johnson said it that way many times, but he also expressed it more colorfully (and more characteristically): "If you let a bully come into your yard one day, the next day he'll be on your porch. And the day after that he'll rape your wife and daughters in your own bed."

His first important decision on Vietnam was to approve a document for circulation inside the government affirming that the policy of the Kennedy Administration would remain the policy of the new Administration as well: "to assist the people and government [of South Vietnam] to win their contest against the externally directed and supported Communist conspiracy."

In his State of the Union Address, he declared: "This nation will keep its commitments, from South Vietnam to West Berlin."

There was never any serious question in the minds of the American people that this forceful figure who was shaping the Presidency to his size would run for election in his own right in November. The only question appears to have taken form in the mind of Johnson himself. Not many were aware of it, but in his memoirs he revealed that "grave doubts" had plagued him despite the popularity he was enjoying.

If one of the facets of his complex personality was an abundant and finely tuned intelligence, another was a strong and often baffling sensitivity (which some saw as insecurity). He did not believe, he said in his account of the Presidency, "that the nation would unite indefinitely behind any Southerner," largely because "the metropolitan press of the Eastern Seaboard would never permit it." Already, he said, he had had enough "of the derisive articles about my style, my clothes, my manners, my accent and my family...to last a lifetime."

He was conscious, too, as he related it, of his "constant uncertainty" about his health, having sustained a massive heart attack nine years before.

"All these considerations," he said, "made retirement look exceedingly welcome. I felt a strong inclination to go back to Texas while there still was time..."

However strong that inclination might have remained, it was dispelled, partly as the result of two remarkable letters to him from his wife, Lady Bird. In one she said that to step out would be "wrong for your country and I can see nothing but a lonely wasteland for your future." In the other she advised him to go for it, recognizing that "you and I—and the children—will certainly get criticized," but to do the best he could—for one term only, at the end of which time "I believe the juices of life will be stilled enough..."

The major question in the public's mind—and eventually in the President's —centered on his running mate.

Almost from the beginning there had been speculation whether the Vice Presidency would go to Robert Kennedy, who had stayed in Johnson's Cabinet as Attorney General, as he had been in his brother's.

Johnson had enjoyed relations ranging from cordial to warm with most of the Kennedy family. In the Senate he had been John Kennedy's senior, but he served him loyally as Vice President and both respected and admired him. As Vice President he had had a pleasant association with Jacqueline Kennedy; he had been solicitous of her welfare and attentive to her needs in the aftermath of the assassination, and she had responded warmly. ("Thank you for walking yesterday behind Jack," she wrote the day after the funeral. "Thank you for the way you have always treated me...We were friends, all four of us.")

Only with Robert Kennedy—who had protested Johnson's position on the ticket in 1960 and ignored him throughout the Kennedy Administration—had there been friction. "I doubt," Johnson said later, "[that we] would have arrived at genuine friendship if we had worked together a lifetime. Too much separated

Vietnam casts a cloud over the campaign, although it does not seem particularly threatening at the time. (top) The President announces retaliation against North Vietnam for its attack on two American destroyers in the Gulf of Tonkin. (above) Dedicating a dam in Oklahoma, the President says of the situation in Vietnam: "We don't want our American boys to do the fighting for Asian boys. We don't want to get involved in a nation with 700 million people and get tied down in a land war in Asia." It is one of several such statements he makes in the course of his campaign, all of which will haunt his Presidency.

us—too much history, too many differences in temperament." For his part, Kennedy made no secret of his dislike for Johnson—but he did want second place on the ticket with him in 1964.

There was considerable agitation on the part of some of Kennedy's friends to get it for him. The President defused that boomlet with a stratagem that seemed transparent, even duplicitous to many. Professing to discern similar swells of support for other officials, he announced that, rather than have his government distracted by such campaigns, no Cabinet officer would be eligible for the Vice Presidential spot. Kennedy said, "I'm sorry to take so many good guys over the side with me." Later that year, he sought Johnson's advice about running for the Senate in New York and received the President's strong support: "I think from the overall national standpoint, my standpoint, and the party standpoint, it would be desirable...I think you could win it hands down."

The day the Democratic convention opened in Atlantic City, Johnson's choice for his running mate was revealed to be Hubert Humphrey. In the Senate, the two men had forged a working relationship based on a mutual regard for each other's abilities that was mutually beneficial as well, Johnson guiding Humphrey from being a maverick outsider to membership in the rank of effective leaders, Humphrey working to keep Johnson's ties to the liberal camp in good order. There was an affection between them, too, that would continue despite differences in temperament and the tensions of the time they shared. "They are good foils for each other," Lady Bird said. Johnson once complained that he would like to "breed [the talkative Humphrey] to Calvin Coolidge." And Humphrey, ebullient to the end, would say after Johnson's death: "Sometimes I would stir up a little trouble just to get loved up again."

They were nominated by enthusiastic acclamation.

The momentum of the campaign was with Johnson from the start. The Republican nominee, Senator Barry Goldwater, had staked out an unyielding position on the right, seeming to be antagonistic to such widely accepted institutions as Social Security and TVA, finding fault with the constitutionality of the civil rights law just passed, stirring fear that he would be somehow lax about the use of nuclear weapons. Part of Johnson's support was clearly a reaction against his opponent's rigidity. But LBJ did not wage a cautious campaign, as he might well have done under the circumstances. Instead, he set out across the country with zest, to obtain a mandate for the social reforms encompassed in his Great Society plans.

The shadow of Vietnam fell twice over the electioneering: once, when the Administration responded to what it reported were North Vietnamese attacks on two U.S. ships legitimately plying the international waters off the Gulf of Tonkin. It secured from Congress a resolution giving Congressional support for the President to "take all necessary measures to repel any armed attack against the forces of the United States and to prevent further aggression."

The other was actually a half-dozen speeches across the country in which the President pledged that he would not "send American boys halfway around the world to do a job that Asian boys ought to be doing for themselves."

Both shadows would haunt his Presidency. The Tonkin Gulf Resolution sailed through Congress with only two dissenting votes; but in the coming months, many of the Senators who had voted for it—including William Fulbright, who had sponsored it—would claim they had been deceived by Administration officials. Their charges of deception would be supported later by writers maintaining that the attacks never took place at all, or, if they did, that they had been deliberately provoked by the Americans who were searching for an incident that would spur the kind of resolution they got from the Senate. Members of the Administration would, of course, respond to the charges. "We certainly believed," National Security Adviser McGeorge Bundy said later, "that things were as we represented them to the public." His brother, William Bundy, who had been Assistant Secretary of State for Far Eastern Affairs at the time of the attacks, considered it possible, in retrospect, that the North Vietnamese could have *thought* they were being provoked, but that "nothing of that kind was ever in the minds of members of the administration." George Reedy, whose *Lyndon B. Johnson: A Memoir* was hardly a valentine to his former boss, firmly rebutted the accusations. "I was in the White House [at the time]," he wrote, "and I know I and all my colleagues were all convinced that the crisis was real. If it was a put-up job, this was a fact known only to the President and two or three other people. And while he was a good actor, he wasn't *that* good." Neither fresh charges nor new defenses would settle the matter, and the controversy, fought out in books and classrooms, would continue a generation beyond.

All that was in the future, however. At the time, the shadows could hardly be perceived as dangerous at all. The country was solidly with Johnson, and in November it gave him the biggest victory it had ever given a candidate for President.

A happy First Lady hears the landslide election returns at the Driskill Hotel in Austin, Texas. This would be LBJ's greatest electoral victory, and his last.

(following pages)
The victors begin their new Administration on horseback at the LBJ Ranch, where, just before Christmas, the President welcomes Defense Secretary McNamara, but not his news: Vietnam, which is still only one problem among many, will soon become a Presidential preoccupation.

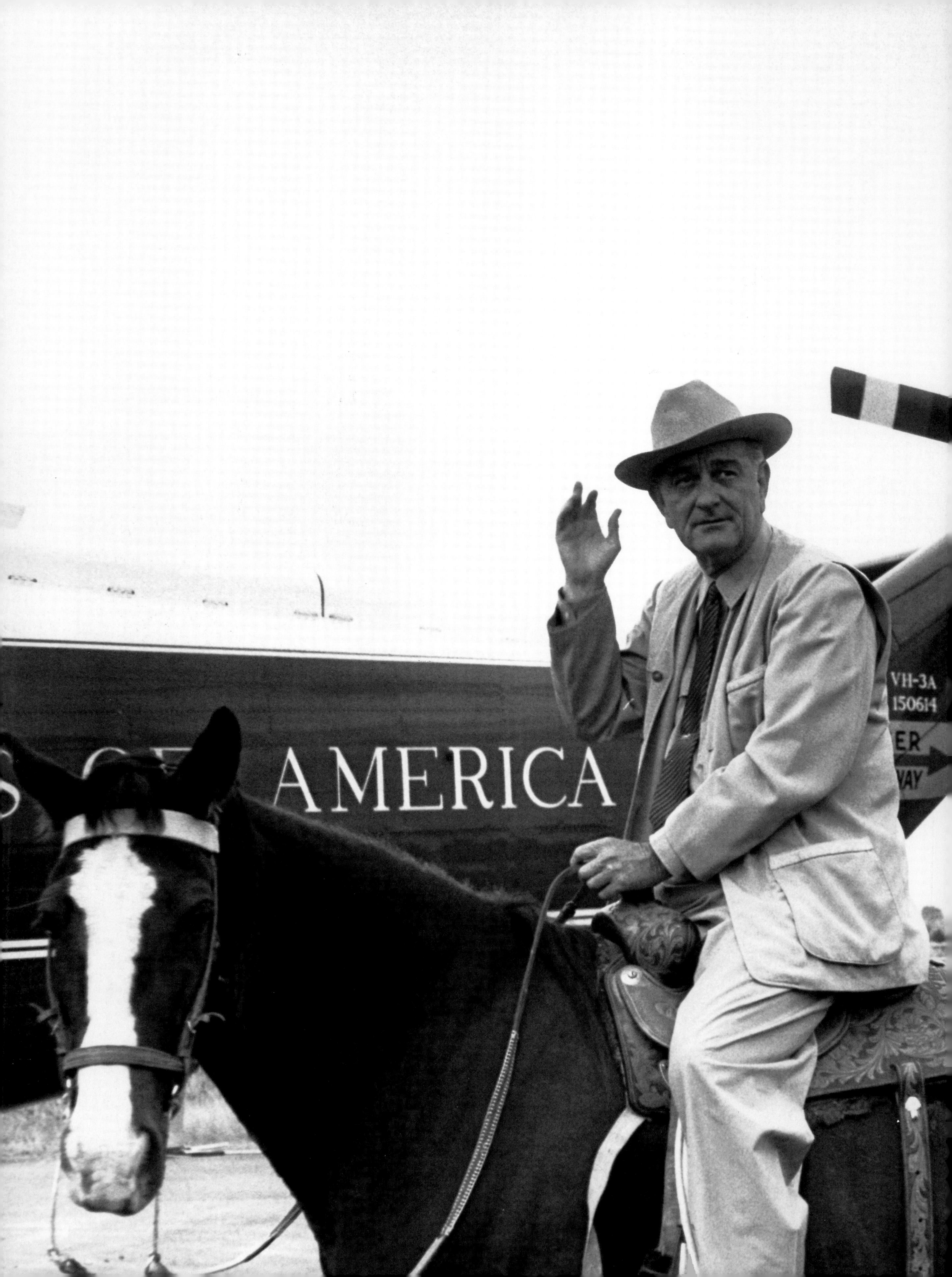
AMERICA
VH-3A
150614

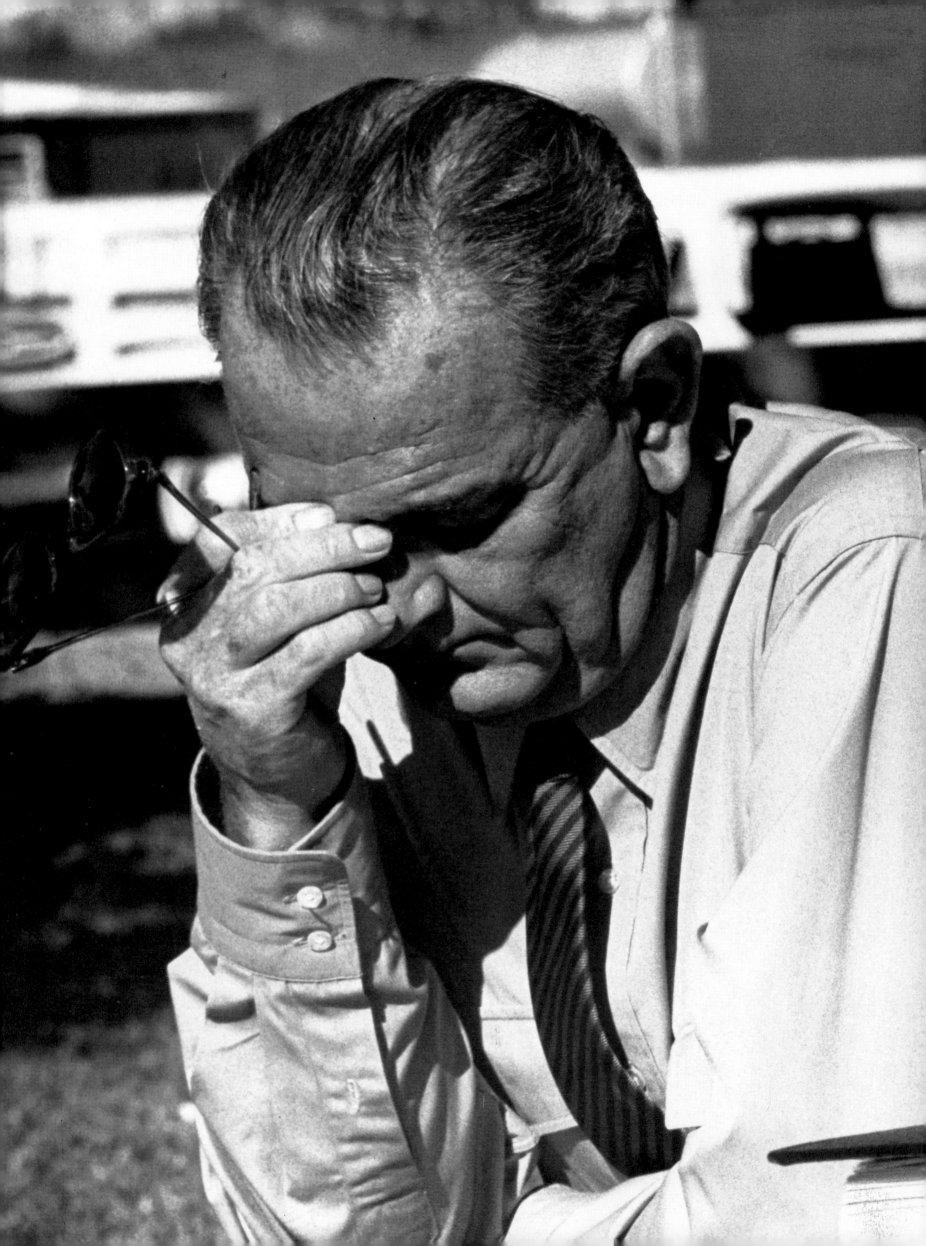

# THE RANCH

I n 1951, the Johnsons bought from his widowed aunt a 250-acre ranch 20 miles west of Johnson City, where he had grown up. It was renamed the "LBJ," additions expanded the original 60-year-old structure, and a swimming pool was carved out in the side yard; but it retained the simple, rustic look of a working Texas ranch, which it was, stocked with herds of white-faced Hereford cattle. It sat on the banks of the Pedernales River, which furnished the water for an irrigation system that Johnson installed to make the ranch an oasis in an arid country.

To Johnson, the place—which had served as a family gathering site at Christmas and other holidays and which he remembered fondly—immediately became home. He returned to it as often as he could, and to the satisfactions of statecraft in his life were now added the deep-reaching pleasures of ranching. "For me, it means continuity, permanence and roots," Lady Bird said. "For Lyndon it means surcease from problems. Of

course, the President's problems follow him from the Potomac to the Pedernales, but here he can become a rancher again for a few hours. Along about sunset, he is likely to call to me, 'Come on, let's go see the deer.'"

Political leaders and foreign visitors—including West Germany's Chancellor Konrad Adenauer and Mexico's President Adolfo Lopez-Mateos—began making pilgrimages to the ranch when Johnson was Senate majority leader. When he was Vice President, the astronauts who were beginning the exploration of space and who were then the country's special heroes carved their names in stepping stones leading to the house. The month after he became President, the state visit of West Germany's new Chancellor Ludwig Erhard was made there, and from then on, for the next five years, the LBJ Ranch was the Western White House, where foreign dignitaries were entertained, advisers consulted, affairs of state were conducted, and the Texas hill country was opened to the eyes of the world.

Lady Bird Johnson holds the family Bible as her husband is inaugurated as President in his own right. Later, they lead the dancing at a gala Inaugural Ball.

The cartoon showed Lyndon Johnson in pajamas and robe, arms flung wide, standing before an open window, exclaiming, "I'm up, world—ready or not." Drawn by John Fischetti and originally distributed by Publishers Newspaper Syndicate, it was reproduced in *Time* magazine's January 1, 1965 issue because it captured so aptly the relationship that existed between the nation and its overpowering, dominating, number-one citizen as the new year began.

With his election victory he had brought in 38 new Democratic Congressmen and two Senators (including Robert Kennedy of New York), giving Capitol Hill its largest Democratic majority since 1936.

He asked the new Congress for swift enactment of the social programs for which he—and they—had campaigned. His relationship with Congress and with the country at large was at its peak. The road ahead seemed open and unencumbered. "We're on our way now to a Great Society," Martin Luther King, Jr. exuberantly told him.

But the troubles were waiting. Throughout 1964, Johnson had made no substantive change in the policy toward Vietnam. But his advisers believed that "we had been living on borrowed time," as McGeorge Bundy put it, and if the commitment he had pledged to follow through was to be honored, the need for change was urgent. Soon after the inauguration, Bundy set forth in a memorandum his view and that of Defense Secretary Robert McNamara that "our current policy can lead only to disastrous defeat." In the light of growing Communist strength in South Vietnam, they believed the only way to forestall such defeat was "to use our military power…to force a change of Communist policy."

The Communist forces had blown up a building housing U.S. servicemen in Saigon just before Christmas. Now, as if to underscore the seriousness of the Bundy-McNamara alarm, over a period of several days they attacked two other barracks and a U.S. helicopter base, altogether killing and wounding almost 200 American soldiers.

So now before the President was a recommendation to initiate a program of "sustained reprisal"—selective bombing of military targets in North Vietnam —in response to "the whole campaign of violence and terror in the South." Such a program of punishment, the proposal said, would offer "the best available way of increasing our chance of success in Vietnam."

Lyndon Johnson's motto was: No job too big and none too small. I got the first clue of what he meant in the spring of 1964, when the hills of his ranch were alive with reporters wanting to know everything about LBJ, the new President and Texas rancher. As cameras ground away, he accommodated them by posing in the pasture with his cattle. He was already disgusted that the press invariably photographed his "bad" cattle and never his best white-faced Herefords. And he didn't want that to happen again.

As we watched this pastoral interview, he spied me just standing there, doing nothing. If there was one thing Johnson couldn't stand, it was idle hands. "Shoo those good cattle on up here," he shouted, and I found myself behind a 2,000-pound bull, saying "shoo, shoo, shoo." The ranch foreman was standing nearby grinning, "Isn't it wonderful to occupy a high policy position in Washington?"

—LIZ CARPENTER

All of the President's advisers supported the recommendation. After three days of deliberation, he approved it.

Bundy, who had drafted the recommendation, appended to it a "final word": "At its very best, the struggle in Vietnam will be long," but "it is our belief that the people of the United States have the necessary will to accept and to execute a policy that rests upon the reality that there is no shortcut to success in South Vietnam."

Later, after Johnson had left the White House, Bundy would reflect: "I didn't have a specific term [in mind]; neither could I have said in early 1965 that we'd still be bombing three and a half years later...I don't think any of us thought or believed that it would be that long, that inconclusive, and that big..."

When the bombing began, the first stirrings of dissent could be felt, and heard. Compared with what would come later, they were relatively mild, but Johnson seemed to hear them grow. He was in a hurry to get his domestic program presented to the Congress in draft legislation, and enacted. He called together the members of the various departments of government who were handling legislation. Wilbur Cohen, then Assistant Secretary of Health, Education and Welfare, was in that assembly, and as he remembered it: "The President said to us: 'Now, look, I've just been reelected by an overwhelming majority, but I want to tell you that every day while I'm in office I'm going to lose votes. I'm going to alienate somebody. It's going to be Vietnam or something else, but it's going to be something.' And he said, 'We've got to get this legislation fast. We've got to get it during my honeymoon.'" It was much the same in the White House. "He would stick his head in our offices," Moyers recalled, "and say, 'Boys, get that legislation up there,' or 'Boys, get that call made, because we don't have much time.'" "He used that period of four or five months to push us as hard as possible," Cohen said. "I never worked so hard in my life as I did between February and June of 1965."

Johnson considered the 1964 Civil Rights Act to be the greatest achievement of his Administration to that point. But he regarded his effort to get it passed as a tribute to John Kennedy. Now he wanted to move on. "I had some dreams of my own," he later said. A successful product of the political system himself, he had total confidence in the power of the ballot. What he wanted was a law that would assure all Americans their constitutional right to vote, eliminating the artificial and usually ridiculous barriers that had been traditionally erected in some states to prevent black citizens from going to the polls. The requirement should be only "age and the ability to read and write," he said, "no tests on what Chaucer said or Browning's poetry or memorizing the Constitution."

He sought the aid of the leaders of the civil rights movement. A voting rights act, he told them, would be a greater breakthrough than the 1964 act with its sweeping provision of access to public accommodations because "it will do things that even that act couldn't do." To King, he said: "Nothing will be as effective as getting all Negroes voting. That will deliver a message that all the eloquence in the world won't bring because the fellow will be coming to you then instead of you calling him."

Help came in a way that could not have been foreseen. A march in Alabama to dramatize the disenfranchisement of black people in that state was set upon outside Selma by mobs and state troopers with gas and clubs and whips in a confrontation destined to become etched in the nation's memory.

Riding the crest of public horror and indignation at the brutality and terror unleashed against the marchers, Johnson went before the Congress to make one of the most impassioned speeches of his career. "At times," he said, with the country's attention full upon him, "history and fate meet at a single time in a single place to shape a turning point in man's unending search for freedom... So it was last week in Selma, Alabama." His call for a law to guarantee every person's right to vote was directed at both the country's conscience and its

Beginning his full term, LBJ claims spiritual kinship with both President Franklin Roosevelt, with whom he shares belief in a compassionate, activist government, and the late Speaker of the House, Sam Rayburn, master of the art of compromise and the search for a common ground.

**Early in 1965, McGeorge Bundy**
(back to the camera), **National Security Adviser,
tells the President that more
U.S. involvement is needed in Vietnam.**

(left)
**A group of advisers from
outside government,
known as the "Wise Men,"
counsel the President on Vietnam policy
throughout his Administration.
They include** (from the top) **General Omar Bradley,
John J. McCloy, Arthur Dean, and** (opposite)
**former Secretary of State Dean Acheson.**

sense of the significance of the moment: "Rarely in any time does an issue lay bare the secret heart of America itself…The issue of equal rights for American Negroes is such an issue." "No one coughed, no one whispered," *Time* reported, as the President approached the climax of his message. Roy Wilkins, head of the NAACP, said later that the galleries were leaning forward, because "the President was beginning to speak as we had heard no President speak before." When he capped his plea for justice with the thundering words of the civil rights movement—"We shall overcome"—the chamber exploded in a roar of affirmation that seemed to signal an end forever to the old order of race relations.

Two months later, Johnson promised the black graduating class at Howard University in Washington that he would carry the fight even further to eliminate the conditions rooted in slavery that denied blacks the same opportunities other citizens had. "We have pursued [the concept of justice] faithfully to the edge of our imperfections," he said, "and we have failed to find it for the American Negro. So it is the glorious opportunity of this generation to end the

**P**eople ask—and the debate will long continue—

what is the reason for our entry into Vietnam?…I know—because of my personal involvement and because

it's been a subject of enormous interest to me ever since—I know why we got in. I can see it, I can feel it, so

that at least in my own mind I have no doubt about it.

Think back to the Second World War. Hitler went on the march. We sat back, as did the other free nations

of the world, and we did nothing. He moved into one nation after another, taking them over. When it was

over, and we had fought the most terrible war in history, my generation had a curious feeling of guilt—that

in some manner we had let our people down. Because we could have moved if we had had the knowledge, if

we had had the wit, if we had had the resolution, we could have moved at any one of those stages and

stopped Hitler and prevented the war that led to the deaths of tens of millions of human beings and hun-

dreds of billions of the world's treasure. So we had this strong feeling—we must never do that again. We had

learned a very serious lesson…

*So, when the situation began in Southeast Asia, that was in the minds of our country's leaders. We must move now. We must not wait. Communism is on the march. It looked at that time as though there was this monolithic conspiracy between the Soviet Union and Red China to move, and at that particular time, it looked as though the move into South Vietnam was just the first step in the takeover of that very important part of the world.*

*As we try to analyze what happened after that, I do not know…what the ultimate result will be. I believe that there were great accomplishments from it…Maybe countries like Indonesia would have gone Communist. Maybe had we not been there, things would have happened in India. Maybe something would have happened in the Philippines. By our presence there, it is at least possible that benefit accrued. On the other hand, the price was high. The price in loss of life, the price in loss of treasury, the divisiveness that occurred at home was very substantial. History will later write the story.*

—CLARK CLIFFORD

I was 23 years old when I was accepted into the

first class of White House Fellows—an LBJ program designed to give a group of young people a one-year

apprenticeship at the highest levels of the Federal Government. I wound up staying at the White House four

years, serving as assistant to two splendid press secretaries, Bill Moyers and George Christian. That in itself

was an exciting enough experience, but President Johnson made it even more remarkable by having me

attend many of his White House meetings to take the official notes—three years out of the University of

Georgia and I was recording affairs of state, issues of peace and war. These were years that would never be

repeated or forgotten, when the gates opened for me to the world where history is made, and when we saw

both triumph and tragedy affect a President's life and a nation's future.

—TOM JOHNSON

one huge wrong of the American nation and, in so doing, to find America for ourselves, with the same immense thrill of discovery which gripped those who first began to realize that here, at last, was a home for freedom."

In a press conference soon thereafter, he was asked the question that had been hovering in many minds for more than a year: how did his passion for equal justice square with those votes against proposed civil rights legislation he had cast in Congress? He answered slowly: "At this stage of the twentieth century there is much that should have been done that has not been done. There will be much to be done in the years ahead. It is a very acute problem and one that I want to do my best to solve in the limited time that I am allowed. I did not have that responsibility in the years past, and I did not feel it to the extent that I do today. I am going to provide all the leadership I can, notwithstanding the fact that someone may point to a mistake or a hundred mistakes that I made in my past."

Later that night he told his staff: "Eisenhower used to call this place a prison. I have never felt freer."

In April, an attempted revolution in the Dominican Republic prompted him to send in 22,000 troops, first to protect and evacuate Americans, and then, as the rioting appeared to get out of control and the Administration saw the threat of a Communist takeover, "to prevent another Cuba." He was accused of overreaction by some, and he fueled the criticism with a vivid but unverifiable description of the situation in the capital city of Santo Domingo. But in general, the American public approved his response to what could have been a dangerous situation; and when the troops were removed a month later, order had been restored, free elections had been scheduled, and no second Cuba had sprouted up in the Caribbean.

"They are rolling the bills out of Congress these days the way Detroit turns out super-sleek souped-up autos off the assembly line," Tom Wicker reported in his column in the New York *Times*. And so they came through the legislative hopper that active year: Federal help to provide teachers and textbooks and classrooms for schoolchildren and to make it possible for new millions to get a college education; Medicare for senior citizens; voting rights for blacks; new life and recognition for the arts and humanities; assistance to the cities; liberalized immigration; beautification of the nation's highways; purification of polluted water; funds for medical research; and some 600 other public laws to improve the quality of American life. Johnson called it "the greatest session in the history of the U.S. Congress."

He considered these legislative victories to be in the long tradition of government operating at its best—helping people—and he treated them with a sense of drama: he signed the education bills in the one-room schoolhouse where his own education had begun, and in the college from which he had graduated. He went to Independence, Missouri, to put his signature on Medicare in the presence of Harry Truman, whose efforts on behalf of such a bill 20 years before had been branded "socialized medicine." He signed the Voting Rights Act in the Rotunda of the Capitol, and the immigration law in the shadow of the Statue of Liberty. He carried his penchant for the dramatic even to Cabinet appointments, swearing in Lawrence O'Brien as Postmaster General in front of the post office in Hye, Texas, a spot in the road near his birthplace where, he said, he had mailed his first letter. (To give the Cabinet spot to O'Brien, he had persuaded the incumbent, John Gronouski, to become Ambassador to Poland by emphasizing Poland's importance as a listening post to the Communist world. "Fifty years from now, people won't give a damn whether or not you sold a stamp," he told Gronouski, "but they'll care whether you helped to preserve the peace.")

Since the bombing decision in February, the President had tried to make clear—to Americans, to the North Vietnamese, to the rest of the world—that

One of the first press flaps of the Johnson Presidency occurred when photographer Charles Gorry captured LBJ holding his pet beagle up by his ears. (below) A year later, at a White House ceremony honoring prizewinning news photos, the President jokingly asks Gorry: "How much did they pay you to take that one?"

"If you want us there for the landing, be sure to include us in the take-off." Senator Arthur Vandenberg's admonition to President Truman during the Korean war is remembered by Johnson and his advisers.
In the East Room of the White House,
Defense Secretary McNamara prepares for one of the many Congressional briefings on Vietnam that would be held throughout LBJ's Presidency.

**G**eorge Wallace sat down—he's all prepared, you know, to be combative. And Lyndon Johnson—in very characteristic fashion—was in his rocking chair, and he drew it up close to Wallace, and he reached out and put his hand on Wallace's knee—which was a favorite approach of his. "And George, why are you doing this? You ought not," he said. "You came into office a liberal—you spent all your life wanting to do things for the poor. Now why are you working on this—why are you off on this black thing?" He said, "You ought to be down there calling for help for Aunt Susie in the nursing home." And he went through all this catalogue of populist things, and he had Wallace in—in tears.

—HORACE BUSBY

the sole purpose of U.S. involvement in Vietnam was to persuade Hanoi, capital and seat of North Vietnam's government, that it would not be allowed to conquer its neighbor. We did not want territory, he said, nor did we want the overthrow of Hanoi's government; we simply wanted South Vietnam to be left free to create whatever nation it could for itself without interference. If peace were restored, he pledged to provide funds for the industrial development of the Mekong River system, in whose benefits both North and South Vietnam would share.

Neither his assurances nor his offer had any effect on Hanoi.

Nor did the level of warfare in the South decrease with the bombing in the North; instead, it expanded. Hanoi was now sending regular forces down to fight as units. The balance was heavily against Saigon, burdened with a weakened economy and a government assaulted by a series of coups. McNamara came back from Vietnam in July with a gloomy assessment: "The situation in South Vietnam is worse than a year ago (when it was worse than a year before that)."

And now the President was faced with what he clearly understood would be "by far the hardest decision" on Vietnam. Once again the proposition put to him had an "only" in it: only by introducing American ground forces into the fighting was there a hope of avoiding a Communist victory.

Later, in his retirement, Johnson said: "I was pulled kicking and screaming into that war." Even allowing for hyperbole, the statement reveals the anguished frustration of a President launching a great social reform movement, forced to divert his attention to a fire half the world away, which, if left untended, would, as he saw it, eventually involve the United States in an even larger conflagration.

He rejected recommendations from the military for levels of action that he feared would bring China or Russia into the conflict. "I don't want World War III," he protested.

From a few in the Congress and from two in his inner circle of advisers he heard the voice of caution. George Ball, Under Secretary of State, who would henceforth play devil's advocate in discussions on Vietnam, had "grave apprehensions that we can't win." Clark Clifford, an old friend who would eventually replace McNamara as Secretary of Defense, echoed that foreboding: "I don't believe we can win in South Vietnam. If we send in 100,000 more men, the North Vietnamese will meet us...I can't see anything but catastrophe for my country."

In the light of subsequent history, that moment of caution seems to take on special significance. What would later appear to be elemental questions hover unspoken: *If they do match us man for man, how many troops are we*

**Flanked by FBI Director J. Edgar Hoover and Attorney General Nicholas Katzenbach, LBJ announces the capture of Ku Klux Klan members suspected of murdering a civil rights worker on the road between Selma and Montgomery, Alabama.**

A revolution in the Dominican Republic, it is feared, might open the way to a Communist takeover of that country. The President ponders the options with U.N. Ambassador Adlai Stevenson. (overleaf) Tense meetings in the halls and offices follow the President's decision to send in American troops. They are withdrawn after a month when order is restored.

**A**t times history and fate meet at a single time in a single place to shape a turning point in man's unending search for freedom. So it was at Lexington and Concord. So it was a century ago at Appomattox. So it was last week in Selma, Alabama.

There, long-suffering men and women peacefully protested the denial of their rights as Americans. Many were brutally assaulted. One good man, a man of God, was killed...

Our duty must be clear to all of us. The Constitution says that no person shall be kept from voting because of his race or his color. We have all sworn an oath before God to support and to defend that Constitution. We must now act in obedience to that oath...

We cannot, we must not, refuse to protect the right of every American to vote in every election that he may desire to participate in.

But even [then], the battle will not be over. What happened in Selma is part of a far larger movement which reaches into every section and state of America. It is the effort of American Negroes to secure for themselves the full blessings of American life.

Their cause must be our cause too. Because it is not just Negroes, but really it is all of us, who must overcome the crippling legacy of bigotry and injustice.

And we shall overcome...

Special Address to the Congress
March 15, 1965

(previous page, left)

**Johnson's determination to improve the lot of black citizens continues to be the centerpiece of his program.**

(previous page, right)

**In the wake of violence against civil rights demonstrators, he seeks new legislation assuring all citizens the right to vote and asks for the help of Martin Luther King in rousing popular support for the legislation.**

(top)

**Johnson enlists the help of civil rights leaders who know how to work with Congress, such as Roy Wilkins.**

(above)

**Assisted by staff members Lawrence O'Brien and Bill Moyers, he tallies the progress of the bill in Congress.**

(opposite)

**When the bill is passed, he signs it in the Rotunda of the Capitol.**

Dramatizing his legislative victories, Johnson signs a bill providing Federal aid to education in front of the schoolhouse he attended, sitting next to the woman who taught him; stands beneath the Statue of Liberty to sign an immigration bill; and signs Medicare into law with President Truman, who first proposed it.

*prepared to commit? How long are we prepared to fight?* But the moment passed, and history turned on the majority advice that the steady application of pressure would force North Vietnam to bargain an end to the war. Later, much later, when he was teaching law in his native Georgia, Secretary of State Dean Rusk would say, in effect: we did not count on the enemy's willingness or ability to keep fighting for as long as it took. All who were involved, including the President, would say, in effect, when they had left the scene: We did not think the American people would lose heart so soon.

But at the time, the questions went unasked and unanswered, and the voices of caution were not persuasive. "The great difficulty in the arguments of those who were against escalation," said Bundy, "was that they weren't able to produce any very good scenario that would be anything but the Americans getting licked and taking the licking." And beyond American defeat—abhorrent enough to Johnson, who said in anguish that he did "not want to be the first President to lose a war"—was the even grimmer prospect set forth by Rusk: "If the Communist world finds out that we will not pursue our commitments to the end, I don't know where they will stay their hand."

So the President, foreseeing—on the strength of his own convictions and the preponderance of advice available to him—a tragic chain of events that would inexorably lead to World War III if he did not act, made his decision. He called a press conference in late July and announced that he was increasing America's fighting strength in Vietnam to 125,000 men. "Additional forces will be needed later," he said, "and they will be sent as requested." He ended on a poignant and painful note: "I do not find it easy to send our finest young men into battle...I know them all, every one...I think I know, too, how their mothers weep and how their families sorrow."

He had already been arising in the night to check on the return of pilots after a bombing run. Now to that hard duty he would add scanning casualty lists from the infantry.

A quarter century later, Bill Moyers privately gave his own insight into Lyndon Johnson as he saw him in that period: through the years he had worked for LBJ, he had watched him go through occasional melancholy periods. The decision to commit troops to Vietnam brought on a despondency that lasted longer than any he had observed before. "He knew better than anyone," Moyers said, "what the cost would be—to his Presidency, to his hopes, to the unity of the country. But he believed in the fiber of his soul that he had to take this course. It was tearing him apart." As he watched the moods come and go with increasing frequency, Moyers recalled, "I thought he would pull out of it, as he always had, but if he didn't I was preparing to talk to Mrs. Johnson." The melancholy mood did lift. The business of government went on.

But the rift the President foresaw was there. The objections that had begun with the bombs of February accelerated after the commitment of troops. LBJ still had the bulk of public opinion with him, but he was losing support from influential sources—including the New York *Times*, which had once described South Vietnam as vital to American interests, and Walter Lippmann, columnist sage of world affairs. There were the first stirrings of the dissent from Martin Luther King that would eventually bring silence to the communication between them. William Fulbright, chairman of the Senate Foreign Relations Committee, moved from his original position of support into full opposition. Open protest had begun in the intellectual community. Some artists invited to a White House ceremony designed to celebrate the importance of the arts in American life used the occasion to show their resistance to White House policy. Demonstrations against the war began to sprout on college campuses and soon were parading through the streets of a dozen cities.

And even though the polls showed public support, the President was finding it difficult to forge an understanding in the public's mind of the grave issues involved, as he saw them. He opened one press conference by reading a letter he had received from a woman who wrote that she could not understand why we were in Vietnam. "I have tried," he said in frustration, "to answer that question dozens of times and more in practically every state of the Union. Let me again, now, discuss it here…"

But the question persisted, despite the answers.

Johnson's faith in the power of education equaled his faith in the ballot. It was the best and surest way out of poverty, and the way to full and productive citizenship for all. Indeed, he thought it should be one of the entitlements of citizenship. "Every child born in America," he said, "has the right to as much education as he or she can take." "Good medical care," too, he believed to be "a right, not just a privilege." He considered the legislative breakthroughs achieved early in the year—Federal aid to education, and Medicare—to be just the beginning. And, in fact, before he left the White House, he would sign 60 education bills in all, and 40 for medical assistance and research. "Green lights went on all over town," said John Gardner, who became Secretary of Health, Education and Welfare in July, "when the President showed that he cared. He really cared, not just today but week after week, month after month, about education and about health. He gave those fields a momentum, and leadership is 70 percent momentum. That's what he supplied."

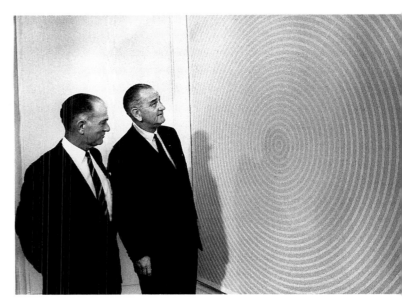

**The Great Society makes the Federal Government, for the first time in American history, a patron of the arts. At a White House arts festival, a bemused President, accompanied by S. Dillon Ripley, Secretary of the Smithsonian Institution, looks at some of the visual works his programs will support.**

**The President inspects flood damage in Minnesota—a bit too closely, it is reported, in the view of the Secret Service.**

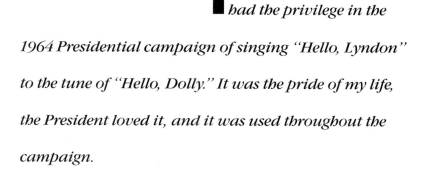

**I** had the privilege in the 1964 Presidential campaign of singing "Hello, Lyndon" to the tune of "Hello, Dolly." It was the pride of my life, the President loved it, and it was used throughout the campaign.

Well, after he was elected, they invited us to an evening in the White House, and I was dancing with the President of the United States. The United States Marine Band started playing and singing "Hello, Dolly"...and President Johnson turned to me and said, "Hey, somebody stole my song!"  —CAROL CHANNING

After decorating astronauts James McDivitt and Edward White, the President says he wants them to travel immediately to Paris, along with their wives and Vice President Humphrey, to represent the United States at an air show. The Johnson women scurry to put together wardrobes for the wives while the President sees the still-startled men off on their journey.

*A*ll those who can remember November 22, 1963 know exactly where they were and what they were doing when they heard of President Kennedy's assassination. I am no exception.

*What is different for me is that my life has never been the same since.*

After a death, people often ask, "What can I do that will be helpful?" I remember the one thing I knew to do while I awaited my parents' return from Texas was to wash my hair. It felt somehow an irreverent act, as if keeping a vigil by the TV was more dutiful—but ultimately I knew the days to come would require me to look my best, and there would be little time to see to that later. I was right.

I greeted my parents at the door when they returned, and there never seemed time to wash my hair in the days that followed.

*What was it really like to be a teenager in the White House?*

It was uniquely thrilling, frustrating, enlightening, demanding, and confusing. It was filled with all the ups and downs of adolescence magnified by the goldfish-bowl existence of a First Family.

My mother's initial advice to me was, "Don't ever do anything you don't want printed on the front page of the paper." This was very sage advice for a politician. My response was that I'd never run for any political offices—only away from them. Such a response only vented my frustration over being public property; it didn't solve the conflict between my desire to be a "normal teenager" and the public's right to know.

My friends, my dates, my birthdays, my grades, my Baptism—everything seemed to be "public property," subject to the judgment of anyone who chose to assess my strengths and weaknesses, and they did...sometimes on the front page of the paper.

In the summer of 1964, with the presidential campaign heating up, my father dealt with my animosity toward politics by appealing to my vanity and my need to be needed. He told me, "Luci, we're in a sinking ship, I'm giving you a bucket. Are you going to help bail by getting out there and doing the campaign job only you can do? I can't manufacture another daughter before November 3rd, so it's you and Lynda or no one."

I covered twenty-six states myself, campaigning in front of groups of 5 to 5,000. I loved it. I was required after every event to report back to Daddy, naming at least three people I'd met and three things that were important to each of them. That accountability in public life was a lesson I savored.

*Before the campaign was over, I had made peace with politics. I had even come to relish the chance to travel and learn and spread the political gospel as I saw it. Through being a part of the process, I'd come to love it, to cherish being an eyewitness to history and to appreciate the special vantage point I'd been given. I had sat on the front row for the signing of the 1964 and 1965 civil rights acts. I had worked in Project Head Start. I'd entertained official groups in the White House.*

*But the desire to be normal was too overpowering. Marriage seemed the only way out of political life for me. I fell in love the summer before my freshman year in college and married a year later and left the White House for Texas—and a normalcy that never quite materialized for me as it does not for any member of a famous family.*

*The legacy of public service was in my veins. Twenty-five years later, I am still working for causes we began then, and I am still closing every day by recounting three new people I've met, three things that are important to them, and what I've learned that day.*

*There are many legacies of Lyndon Baines Johnson.*

—LUCI BAINES JOHNSON

**Y**ou do not take a person who, for years, has been hobbled by chains and liberate him, bring him up to

the starting line of a race, and then say, "You are free to compete with all the others," and

still justly believe that you have been completely fair.

Thus it is not enough just to open the gates of opportunity. All our citizens must have the

ability to walk through those gates.

This is the next and the more profound stage of the battle for civil rights. We seek not just

freedom but opportunity. We seek not just legal equity but human ability, not just equality

as a right and a theory but equality as a fact and equality as a result.

Commencement Address
Howard University
June 4, 1965

President and Mrs. Johnson attend funeral services for Adlai Stevenson, whose death sets in motion a grim chain of events. LBJ offers Stevenson's U.N. post to Arthur Goldberg, who leaves the Supreme Court to accept—something he later says he had been reluctant to do. Johnson then persuades a wary Abe Fortas to take the vacated Court seat and announces the appointment to the press, along with that of John Chancellor to head the Voice of America. Later, Johnson would be defeated in his effort to make Fortas Chief Justice, and scandal would eventually lead to Fortas's resignation.

In October the President gave a special salute to the Congress for its cornucopia of Great Society legislation, and then he went into the hospital to have his gallbladder removed. While he was recuperating, he showed reporters the scar of the operation—and enterprising photographers recorded the moment for history. There was a reason for Johnson's action: he was aware of rumors that he was suffering from something more serious than a diseased gallbladder, and he wanted to dispel the speculation. But that explanation, in the way of explanations immemorial, never got the currency the photograph enjoyed. He might have done better had he given the reason he later gave the White House correspondents during his last weeks in office. In a wonderfully self-deprecatory moment, to the delight of reporters who had been with him so long, he explained then that Sarah McClendon, a Texas correspondent whose questioning of Presidents often approached baiting, had "popped up from behind a tree and demanded: 'You've been in office almost two years now, and what do you have to show for it?'"

Before going back to the ranch to recover from the operation, Lyndon Johnson heard the fiery cries of protest outside the White House gates. To correspondent Henry Fairlie, visiting him in the Oval Office, he said: "You saw those protesters outside carrying the Viet Cong flag. They'll bring me down. But as long as I'm President of the United States, they'll be allowed to parade the Viet Cong flag out there."

In his retirement, his thoughts returned to the youthful voices he had heard, piercing the space between them like swords. "My heart was with the students," he said once on a long ride across his ranch, "although they would never know that, and I don't suppose they would ever believe it. I'd hear those chants—'Hey, hey, LBJ, how many kids did you kill today?'—and I knew there

was a long gulf between them and me which neither one of us could do much about. I was doing what I thought was right, right for them, and right for their country and their future and their children. But they couldn't see that. What we were doing was based on decisions that were made and actions that were taken before some of them were even born, and that's a hard thing to understand. I didn't blame them. They didn't want to get killed in a war, and that's easy to understand. It would be wonderful if there were a way each generation could start off fresh, just wipe the slate clean all around the world and say, OK, the new world begins today. But nobody's ever found a way to do that. There's a continuity in history that's one of our greatest strengths, but maybe it's one of our weaknesses, too. If a young man says, 'You're sending me to Vietnam because of the SEATO treaty, but I wasn't around when you passed the SEATO treaty, and I don't believe in it and I don't think it's right to put my life on the line for decisions that were made by men when I was in my cradle'—well, there's something there to listen to. But it's possible for us to say to young men and women: you're free, you can vote, you can deny the state the right to enter your house, you can speak your mind without fear of prison—and we can say all these things to them because of decisions made and actions taken by men before any of us were born, before our parents and grandparents were born.''

But at the time, no answer seemed possible to the angry voices of a generation he had hoped to reach and help with laws that would make life easier for them than it had been for their fathers.

(following pages)

**Faced with impending surgery, Johnson is counseled by former President Dwight D. Eisenhower, who saw a mild panic on Wall Street when he was hospitalized during his Administration. The result is one of the most widely covered and completely photographed surgeries in history. LBJ continues to work during his recuperation and offers the press a rare glimpse of a Presidential scar. Before leaving Bethesda Naval Hospital, the President and Mrs. Johnson visit wounded servicemen returned from Vietnam.**

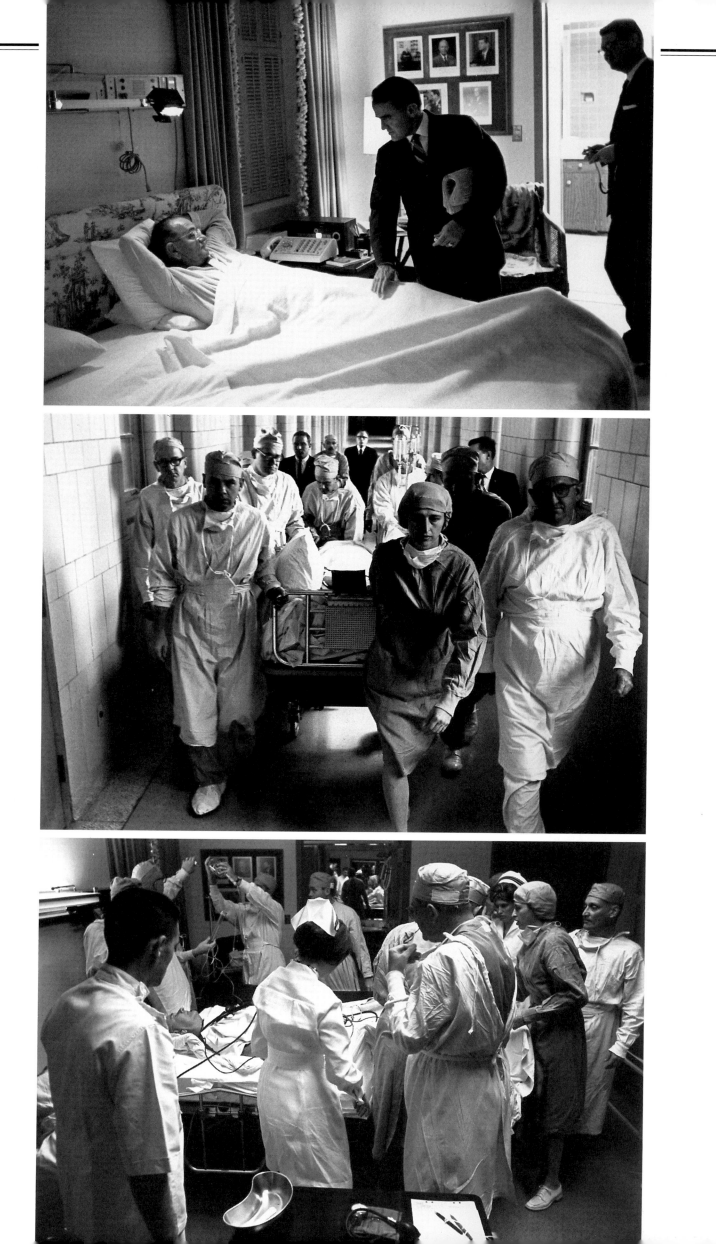

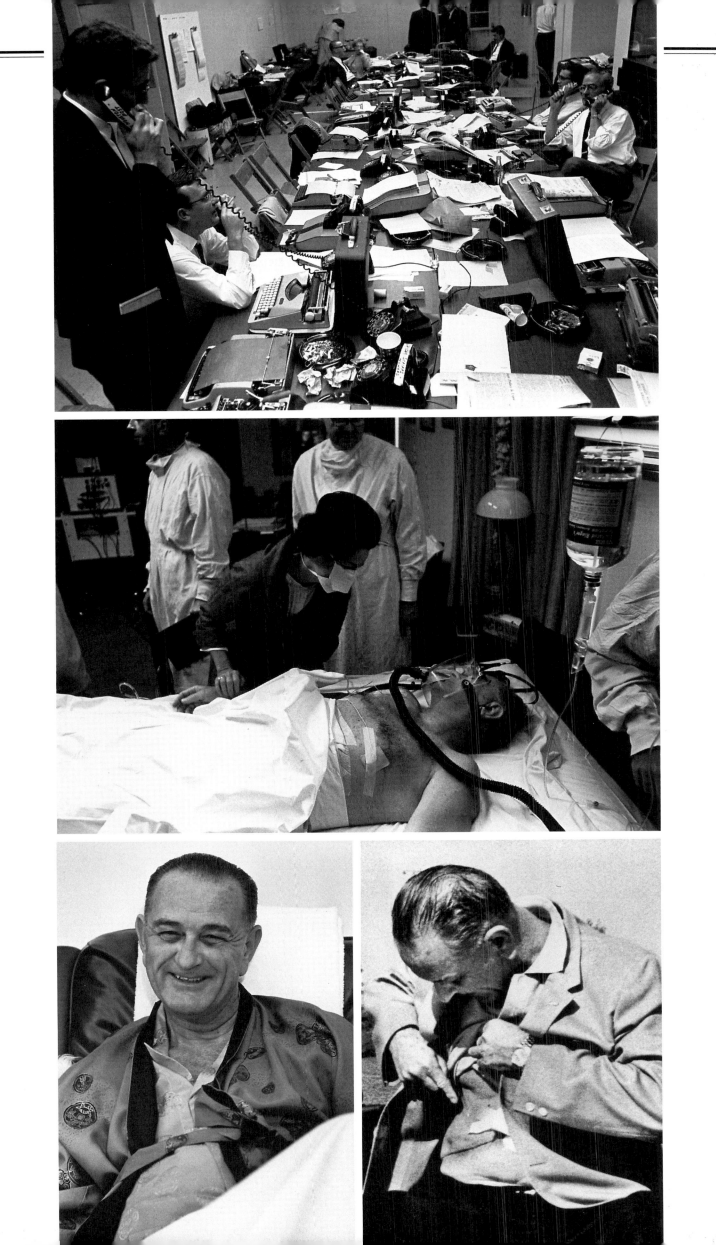

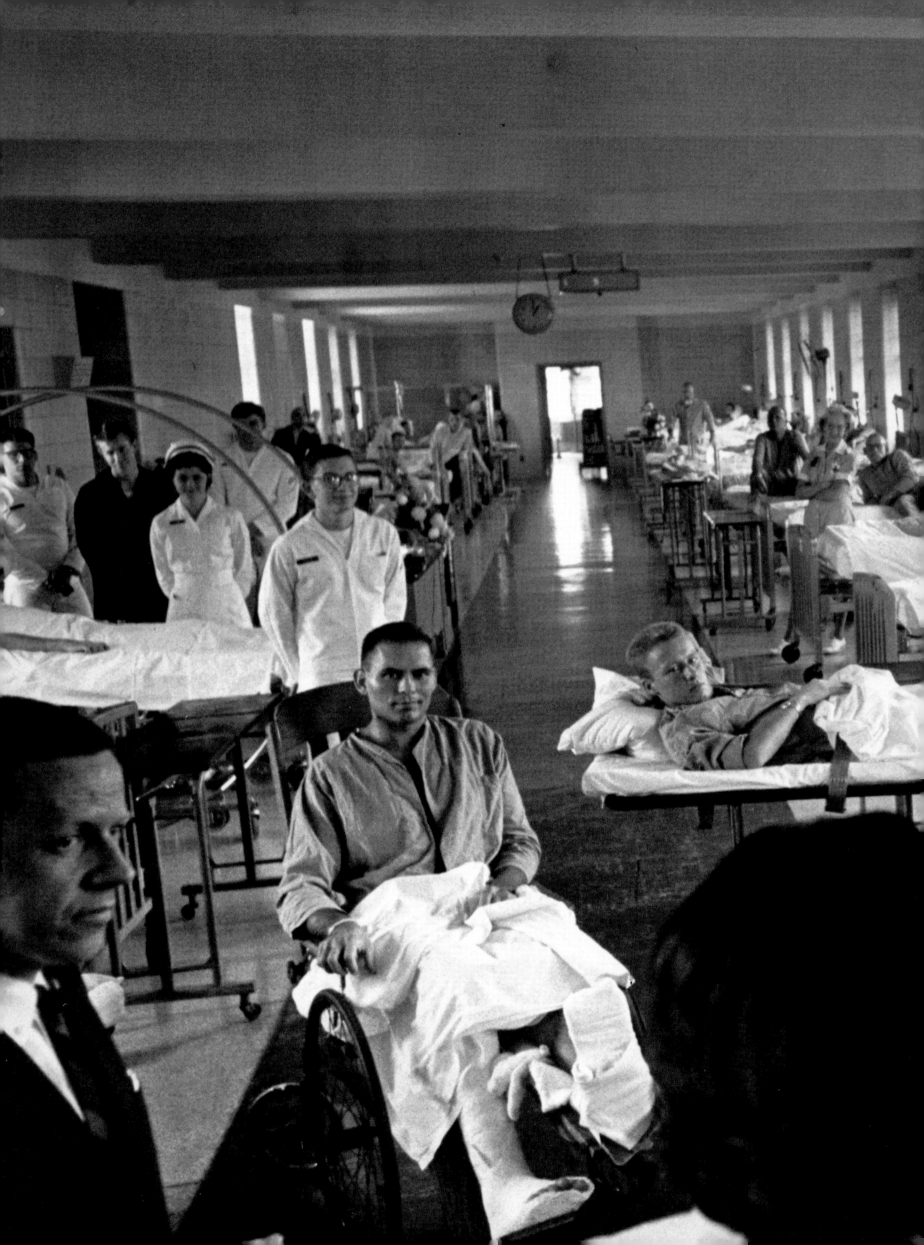

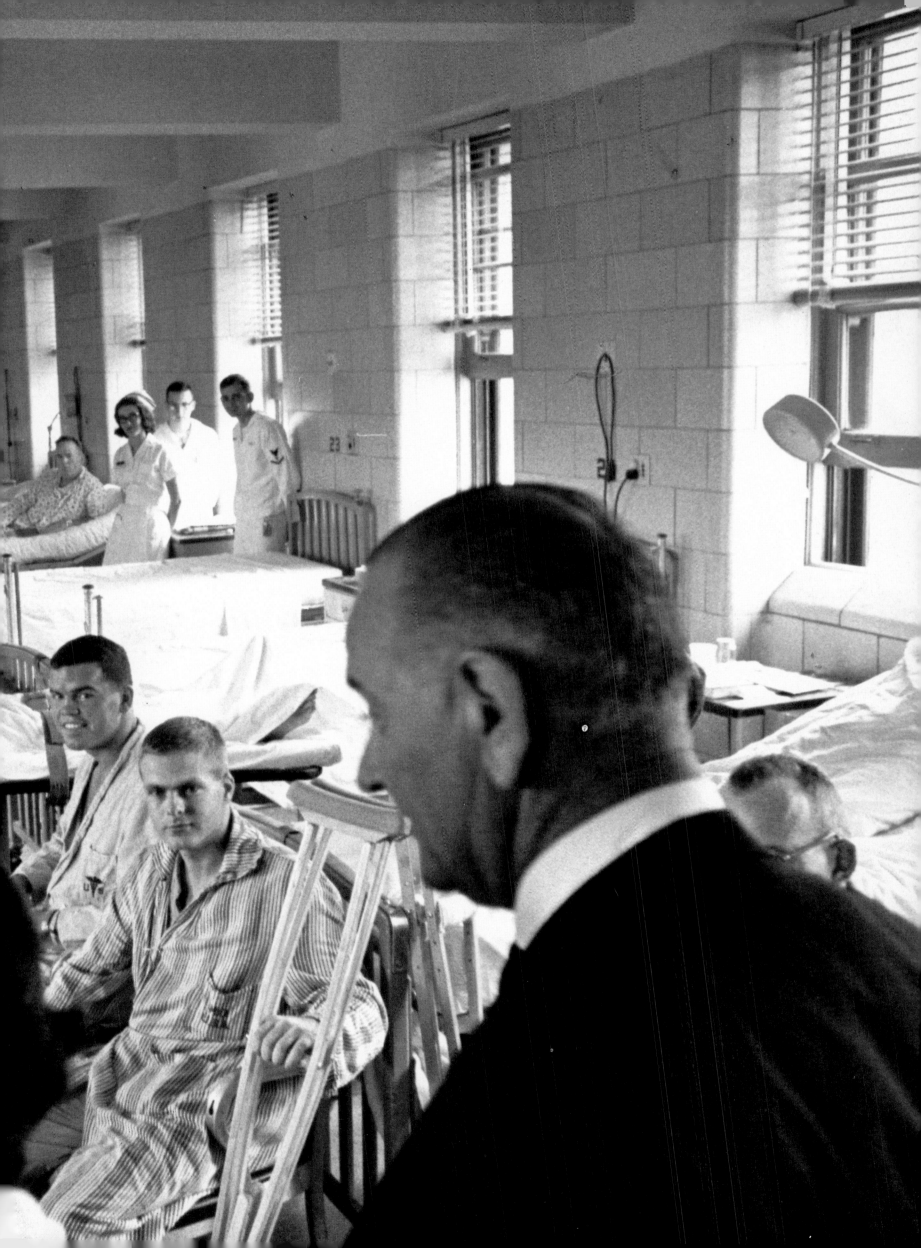

The final social event of the
White House year is a
festive dinner at which the
President amuses Lord Snowdon
and appears to captivate
his wife, Princess Margaret.

# W

ith the legislative victories of 1965 behind him, Johnson was urged to go slow on further reforms. But he was impatient with that advice. "So much more still needed to be done," he said later. After the breakthroughs in education, health, civil rights, and poverty, he was turning his attention now to what he called the "new agenda"—programs to tackle the problems growing out of the special condition of American life at mid-century, which he described as "the growth in population, the massive decay of our cities, the steady separation of man from nature, the depersonalization of life in the post-industrial age..."

He had created a dozen task forces composed of experts in their various fields, from industry and government and universities, to come up with constructive approaches to such problems as transportation, pollution, urban congestion, and protection for the consumer in the marketplace.

So to the surprise of many, his legislative proposals were almost as extensive as the preceding year's.

In a blur of cigarette smoke and fortified
by coffee, the President's staff works
on successive drafts of his 1966
State of the Union Message: a ringing
assertion to Congress that the nation
can pursue the war in Vietnam and build
the Great Society at the same time.

Nor was he disposed to pull back in Vietnam. There was heartening indica-
tion that the change in policy was paying off. The commitment of American
troops, *Time* reported, had brought about a "military standoff" with the Communists—and more: it had "stiffened the spirit of the South Vietnamese" and
"created a new atmosphere of hope and confidence throughout Asia's southern crescent of nations."

At the end of 1965 the President had ordered a temporary halt to the bombing of military targets in the North. It lasted 37 days, during which time he sent
Vice President Humphrey and other senior officials of the Government to the
major capitals of the world to seek their help in persuading North Vietnam to
negotiate an end to the war. Hanoi denounced the trips as "deceptive" and "a
trick." It insisted that the basis for any negotiation must be an acceptance of the
National Liberation Front, parent body of the Viet Cong, as the sole representative of the people of South Vietnam. So it now seemed clear that there would
be no early end to the fighting. To Johnson and his advisers it also seemed clear

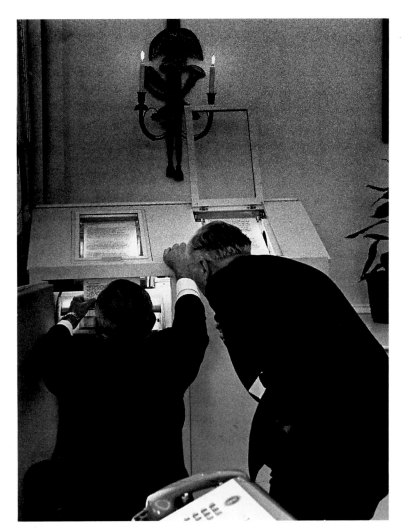

*S*ometimes, in the midst of a meeting, he would walk over and read the latest thing coming out on the ticker. Then he would open the bottom of it—it was in a soundproof cabinet—and would disappear down into the bowels of the thing to read it as it was actually being typed out on the spindle. He wanted to get even farther ahead of the news before it could surface. It was just part of his kind of obsessive communications system.

—DOUGLASS CATER

that the end would come only when Hanoi was persuaded that victory would be forever beyond its reach. Clark Clifford, who, after his earlier caution, supported the Administration's decisions, said: "Until [the North Vietnamese] know they are not going to win, they will not talk." The bombing was resumed.

Although the loudest voices of disagreement with the Administration's Vietnam policy had come from the dovish left, the ones Johnson professed to fear the most were now coming from another source. The concept of a limited war fought for limited aims had angered the hawkish right in the 1950s when it was tested in Korea, and now the effort in Vietnam was summoning that same response. "It would have been easier," Johnson admitted, "to break out the flag for an all-out military effort." But repeating that he neither sought nor wanted a "wider war," he held to the course he had set.

At least, then, said the opposition from the right, domestic activity should be curtailed. Senator Dirksen, the minority leader, summed up their objection: "We've got a war on our hands, and I think some of these programs can be scaled down." He also protested to the managers of the war, "You ask for a billion here, a billion there; pretty soon that adds up to real money."

But the President went all out for guns and butter. "This society," he insisted, "is strong enough to pursue our goals in the rest of the world while still building a Great Society here at home."

So the policy would remain the same: a steady but controlled increase in military pressure, under which the enemy would surely eventually crack. There were now 184,000 American troops in Vietnam, with almost 200,000 more scheduled to go by the end of the year.

The country was enjoying an unprecedented period of sustained economic prosperity. But with the cost of the war accelerating, inflationary pressures were building, and the Council of Economic Advisers thought it would be

**After halting the bombing of North Vietnam for more than a month to encourage negotiations, the President reads news reports of Hanoi's rejection of his overture. With him is Robert Komer, in charge of the Administration's "other war" in Vietnam, the "pacification" effort, aimed at improving life in the countryside, thus making peasants less vulnerable to Communist blandishments.**

*I don't know how many people I've heard, very distinguished people, say after leaving a small meeting with Johnson, "My God, if people could only see him that way." But if you look back over a transcript of what he said in a small meeting, you see that he used arguments and told stories and made analogies that just simply would not do on 30 minutes of television. Sometimes, after touching first base, he goes to left field, climbs into the bleachers, sells hot dogs, runs back down on the field, and circles the bases and comes home. You think he's never going to get to the point. But it all comes back with tremendous force and with great comprehensive power when he ends his argument, and it's damned near irresistible when he's at his best. This can't be done on television.*

—HARRY MCPHERSON

Some members of Congress are
becoming increasingly less receptive
to the President's Vietnam policy.
(center, left) **Senator William Fulbright
will soon break with
the Administration, while**
(center, right) **Mike Mansfield,
Senate majority leader,
will remain friendly and
cooperative even as he voices
his opposition to the war.**

As the war proceeds, one of the
President's saddest jobs is
presenting decorations and
consolations to the widows and
families of men killed in action.

(overleaf)
**Johnson meets with
Nguyen Cao Ky and other
South Vietnamese government
leaders in Honolulu, getting
their agreement on land reforms
and other improvements
for South Vietnam's people.**

(preceding page)

**The Johnson family makes a state visit to Mexico.**
(above) **While there, the President accepts a gift from the young son of Mexican entertainer Cantinflas, in gratitude for Johnson's effort earlier in the year to save the life of the boy's mother by flying her to an American hospital for desperately needed medical treatment.**

prudent to seek a tax increase. When Johnson tested the waters, however, the votes were not there. So the year would pass without a request for increased taxes.

Behind the military effort in the field, Johnson wanted South Vietnam to build not only a strong government, but also a democratic society dedicated to improving the lives of the South Vietnamese people. Nguyen Cao Ky and Nguyen Van Thieu had emerged as leaders from the last coup, Ky as prime minister, Thieu as commander of the armed forces. Their regime had survived for six months, longer than that of any of their predecessors since Diem's assassination in 1963, and thus seemed to offer stability. Johnson met with them both in Honolulu early in the year, and in return for his pledge of constancy to the cause of a free South Vietnam, he extracted the promise that they would work for social justice, land reform, and free elections.

The President suffered his first major legislative defeat when the Congress refused his request to give home rule to the District of Columbia. The District had been governed by Congress from the beginning. Johnson, like other Presidents before him, thought it was something of a travesty to have the very seat of democracy administered like a colony. But many Congressmen traditionally liked the prerogatives that a Federal city gave them, and some undoubtedly did not want to give self-rule to the increasingly black population of Washington. Johnson thought the defeat was a signal of things to come, but in fact, 42 major laws were passed that year, continuing the thrust of his Great Society.

He put the first black into a Presidential Cabinet when he appointed Robert Weaver Secretary of the newly created Department of Housing and Urban

**Bob Hope and Jerry Colonna demonstrate some hoofing for the President before taking their show on the road to U.S. troops overseas.**

*This is my favorite picture of what the most serious side of Washington is. President Johnson was talking to Secretary Rusk and to me about a very difficult decision. Secretary Rusk actually has his hand on his chin, trying to figure out how to execute the President's decision. I had talked separately with them both and knew how difficult it was for the President and also for the Secretary of State. I had enormous compassion for them.*

*But when I came back to academic life, the first question the students would ask when they got comfortable with me was, "Don't you miss power?" And that picture really captures the answer that I tried to give them, which is, if you work closely with a President who has the qualities of Presidents Kennedy and Johnson, what you learn is the difference between responsibility and advice, and what you are conscious of is the enormous gap between the best you can do for the President and his responsibilities to the country and the world and to mankind. So you do your best, but you are made very conscious as you watch him make decisions that your role is not one of power.*

—WALT ROSTOW

Development. Lady Bird Johnson attended the swearing in of the new secretary, and recorded in her dairy: "It was one of those moments when a sense of history hung in the air."

The younger Johnson daughter, 19-year-old Luci, was married that summer to Patrick Nugent, the first daughter of an incumbent President to wed since Eleanor Wilson in 1914. The President told Liz Carpenter, the First Lady's staff director, who was handling the overall press arrangements, that David Dubinsky, head of the International Ladies Garment Workers Union, "cried" when he learned that the bridal dress was being made with nonunion labor. A new gown was quickly put together sporting the proper label, and the President walked his daughter down the aisle of Washington's Shrine of the Immaculate Conception.

A group of Democrats running for Congress met with the President, most of them for the first time. For an hour they heard him give a virtuoso performance excoriating his political opposition, defending his foreign policy, and personalizing his programs. (The new minimum wage bill he had gotten from the Congress was for "the little charwoman who scrubs the floor of that motel" and "the waitress that's got three kids at home, that goes in there in the morning before daylight to be ready to serve coffee when they drop in at six o'clock, and usually stays until dark.") Bob Hardesty was present for the occasion, and as he reported it: "Those candidates...were caught up in a whirlwind of rhetoric and emotions that most of them had seldom experienced. One minute they were roaring with laughter. The next minute they were sitting in a chilled hush, some with tears in their eyes. The next minute they were on their feet, cheering...It was vintage LBJ. He was...hilarious; he was compassionate; he was outrageous..."

To such groups the experience of being with him was electrifying. But in the country at large, public opinion polls revealed that he was losing the huge popularity he had enjoyed. It was not unexpected. "I would look out at a roaring crowd that was totally approving," Lady Bird remembered, "and have both a feeling of warmth and chill. You know it's not going to be possible to keep on like that. You couldn't always live up to what they wanted." Presidential counsel Harry McPherson likened the situation to that of a man who gets a stalled train started after the engineer has died: "His craftiness became a legend. He was lionized. He was just what the country needed. Everyone settled back for the ride. But after [taking] it for granted that the train *should* be running," they forgot the qualities they had admired and began concentrating on the man's flaws. "Good lord, they thought, he's just a fixer, not a leader." The press seemed to be particularly vigilant for evidence of what one journal called "petty deceptions," and the term "credibility gap" was now in general circulation in the media for deceits both real and perceived.

Johnson himself was always philosophical about his popularity, as he was about power. He thought both were, in the words of White House counsel Larry Temple, "much akin to green stamps. He said, 'You've got this popularity, but what value is it if you don't spend it for something worthwhile?' He was always talking about spending it to get some legislation through or some action taken. And once spent, it was gone."

(this page and overleaf)
**His popularity may have crested in 1964, but LBJ is still able to draw massive crowds as he takes to the road on what is billed as a "nonpolitical" tour at the beginning of the 1966 Congressional campaign season. It will be his "last hurrah."**

BACK LBJ
IN VIET NAM

POSTAL
CLERKS
AUXILIARY
THANK
VANCE

OUR
THANKS
VANCE
POSTAL
CLERKS

(this page and overleaf)

**The visit of the Commander in Chief to Fort Campbell, Kentucky, at midyear underscores the fact that this is a nation at war.**

The daughter of White House aide
Jack Valenti, Courtney, who has
virtually unlimited access to
the President, one day slips past
the guards and ends up on LBJ's lap
during a National Security Council
meeting. Secretaries Rusk and
McNamara and adviser Walt Rostow
seem less amused than the President.
Knowing a good story when he has one,
though, Johnson later tells
his press secretary, Bill Moyers,
to "leak" this one.

The wedding of younger daughter
Luci to Patrick Nugent is both
a family occasion and a national event.
"Nobody was invited except the
immediate country," one newswoman
reports. After a flap over a
nonunion-made bridal gown,
an anxious mother, proud father,
and lovely bride give the press and
public the kind of event Americans
delight in from their First Families.

Finally, underlying all other considerations was the public's growing concern over Vietnam.

"Today's writers," Dean Rusk observed, "are inclined to discuss Lyndon Johnson almost solely in terms of Vietnam...The historian will take a broader view and weigh such things as the Consular and Civil Air agreements with the Soviet Union, the Non-Proliferation Treaty, our space treaties, the beginnings of SALT talks." These and other measures moved the two superpowers farther toward a normalization of relations than had been accomplished since the end of the Second World War. There were other successful initiatives as well: the effort to encourage the countries of Latin America and other regions to form common markets and regional institutions for their common good; the beginnings at long last of a try at building bridges to the nations of Eastern Europe; LBJ's determined stand when, virtually alone, he succeeded in bringing about a change in the disastrous farm policy of India; the preservation of the NATO alliance at a critical time; and important measures to stabilize the international monetary system. As Rusk suggested, they are all a substantial and significant part of the record for historians to assess in their accounting of the foreign policy of the Johnson years.

But at the time, in the public's mind certainly, and increasingly to the frustrated President, they were overshadowed by the dominant struggle of the day. "Vietnam," Mrs. Johnson noted, "is about two-thirds of what we talk about these days."

In spite of the progress reported by *Time*, support on the pages of influential metropolitan journals was becoming rare, although it could still be found in smaller newspapers across the country.

To Johnson, his position was plain and could be simply stated: "I sat through 1964, and I did not move a man or machine in there. I did not put a plane or a tank or a human. But they just kept coming, and if I had put them in earlier, I might have had it over with earlier. But all I am putting in now against a good many of my advisers is just the minimum number that General Westmoreland says he needs to hold them." To the Congressional candidates, he was wryly philosophical. "I'm doing the best I can," he said. "It's like the old man in my county that said he felt like a jackass in a hailstorm: he just had to hunker down and take it."

In the fall, the President and First Lady travel
through the Pacific. Highlights of the trip include
(top) a welcome in Hawaii, a native drink in Samoa,
an inspection of Philippine rice growing;
(right) a dance with Imelda Marcos; and (far right) a visit to
a New Zealand sheep ranch; (left and below) a motorcade in
Australia, where paint spattered by a few demonstrators
draws headlines, but cheering crowds, numbering
in the thousands, call, "Good on you, Lyndon."

But his detractors refused to sympathize with his position, or even to understand it, and in his frustration his irritation became more strident. He called his critics "nervous nellies."

The country's growing disaffection with the President's Vietnam policy was amorphous and difficult to categorize. It was fed by many conflicting strands of objection: by the belief that the country should be doing more to win the war; by the conviction that the U.S. was itself the aggressor, intervening in the internal civil war of another country; by a dozen varied viewpoints between those two extremes. Many of the dissidents at this stage had no firm feeling of any kind, but were assaulted by, and were reacting to, a general sense of unease.

No doubt part of this stemmed from the President's inability to define his position sufficiently to rally people to its cause. As had been demonstrated in Korea, that was one of the difficulties of this kind of war. "He was trying," as Harry McPherson put it, "to summon up just enough martial spirit and determination in the people to sustain a limited war, but not so much as to unleash the hounds of passion that would force him to widen it." The effort often produced mixed signals and led to confusion. Lady Bird Johnson summarized the situation cogently: "The temperament of our people seems to be, 'You must get excited, get passionate, fight it, get it over with, or we must pull out.' It is unbearably hard to fight a limited war."

And there was a new dynamic at work: the power of communication in its changing form and function. When *Life* magazine, in 1943, published a photograph of three American soldiers lying dead on the beach of New Guinea—

**The Manila meetings direct the nations assisting in the war in Vietnam to withdraw their troops as soon as North Vietnam does the same.** (above) **LBJ prevails in getting a pledge from all signatories to "conquer hunger, illiteracy and disease."** (right) **Adviser Clark Clifford and U.S. Ambassador Henry Cabot Lodge confer with General William Westmoreland, commander of U.S. troops in Vietnam.**

(overleaf)

**The President makes a surprise visit to the U.S. base at Cam Ranh Bay in South Vietnam, where he meets with General Westmoreland and with the men he has sent overseas to fight the war.**

At the base hospital
at Cam Ranh Bay, LBJ
visits with wounded
soldiers and their
nurses, and gives
awards for bravery
in battle.

departing from the tradition of not showing American casualties that had
prevailed since after the Civil War—a new emotional force was unleashed. By
the time American troops landed in Vietnam, the camera had become consid-
erably more sophisticated and infinitely more powerful. It was commonplace
—but undeniably true—to describe Vietnam as the first war to be fought in the
nation's living rooms. Images of the destruction and ugliness of combat,
repeated in a routine that came to seem almost ceremonial, became part of the
nation's consciousness of Vietnam. The stark vignette of Marines putting the
torch to the thatched huts of Da Nang touched a national nerve, creating shock
and dismay. And all of it together—the continuous impressions of an alien land
and a sad people and dead and dying Americans—contributed to a gathering
disquiet in ways that could never be measured.

In October, with Lady Bird accompanying him, Johnson took off on a colorful and exciting journey through the lands of the Pacific. The central purpose of
the trip was to join a conference of the leaders of seven Pacific nations in Manila
and establish with them a united front on the war in Vietnam.

It was an odyssey to cheer any President's heart, but particularly one who
had begun to feel the pressures of hostility at home. Crowds by the tens of

(overleaf)
**At Seoul, Korea,
it looks as if the
entire nation has
turned out to
extend its welcome.**

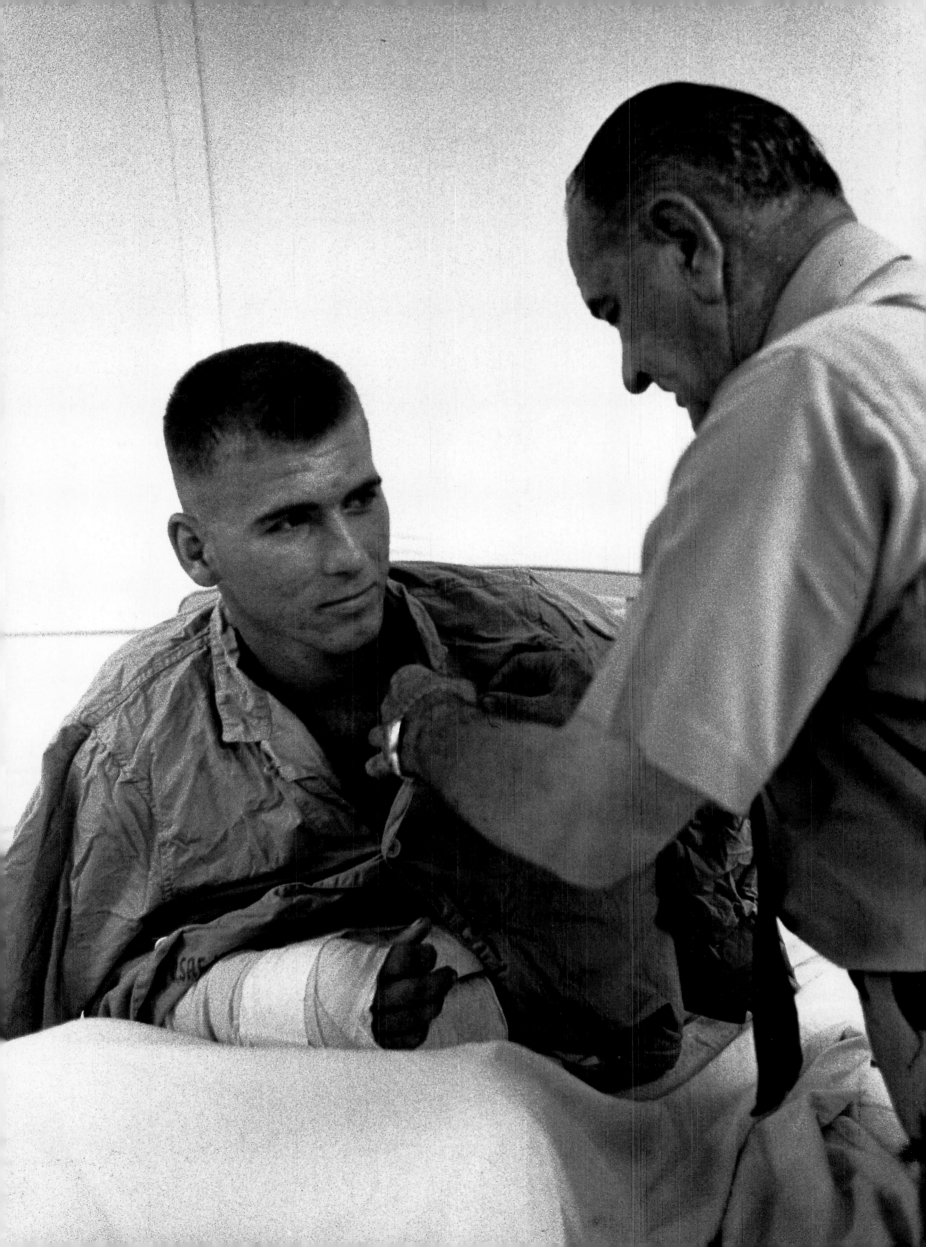

Speaking to servicemen stationed in Korea, an exuberant LBJ cites a grandfather who died at the Alamo. This claim is not true, although he does have a great uncle who fought in the battle of San Jacinto. Later, Johnson will be incredulous at his misstatement, but his unwillingness to admit it publicly leads the press to see the "credibility gap" widen.

thousands lined the streets of Wellington, New Zealand; and in the cities of Australia, where Johnson had been stationed as a naval officer during World War II, the air thundered with cries of "Good on you, Lyndon." In Seoul, capital of South Korea, Harry McPherson noted in his journal: "Looks like they turned out the country." He recorded some of the friendly signs being held aloft: HEY THERE TEX JOHNSON, YOU SURE LOOK FINE and HOWDY COWBOY BIG FRIEND LBJ. Johnson himself, overwhelmed by the mass of humanity, told afterward that through a translator he asked South Korean President Chung Hee Park how big he thought the crowd was. Park put the question to one of the Korean officials in the party. The answer came back: 2 million. Johnson found that staggering. Misinterpreting his expression as criticism, Park apologized. "I'm sorry," he said, "that's all the people we have."

In the course of the journey the President made a surprise trip to be with the soldiers at the American base at Cam Ranh Bay in South Vietnam. It was an encounter that affected him deeply, one that he said he would not forget, and he didn't. Long after, he talked about the "strong hands" that had gripped his, and the "quiet voices" of the wounded he had visited in the hospital.

He went into the hospital himself after that trip, to repair tissue damage left from his gallbladder operation the year before and to have a polyp removed from his throat. Some of the press questioned whether the timing of the operation conveniently relieved him of his implied promise to take to the campaign trail on behalf of Democratic candidates, fearing a rebuff at the polls. Johnson insisted he had not made such a promise, implied or otherwise. "I never wanted to get mixed up in the campaign in the first place," he said later. "I felt bad about it because some of them were people I loved, who had been with me all the way. But I didn't want to get the war mixed up in it." He was aware that plans had been made for his arrival in several cities, but he tried to explain that he always wanted to keep his options open until he had finally decided his course of action. It was a distinction lost to his critics in the media, who considered it a deception—and the "credibility gap" deepened. The Republicans made substantial gains in the election itself.

The President returned to his ranch to recuperate. While he was there he made a trip to Cotulla, Texas, where he had once taught Mexican-American children—an experience that had stayed with him and to which he returned often, in person or in reflection. "I always remembered those kids," he said, "and the hurt look in their eyes that just gets born there when you're poor and you're discriminated against."

He went to San Antonio to meet wounded GIs being returned to Texas from Vietnam and then to the ranch for the holidays. Despite the "miasma of trouble [hanging] over everything," Lady Bird noted, "life goes on, and so does Christmas."

A weary but satisfied President completes his trip.

f Lyndon Johnson had never become President, his daughter Luci said, if he had never gone to Washington at all, he would still have made a considerable reputation for himself in the Texas hill country as a great storyteller—and this in a region where storytellers abound.

It was a part of Johnson that most of the nation never saw. He belonged, Lady Bird said of him, to the age of courthouse politicians, thrust into the hostile world of television. His major addresses were often eloquent and dramatic, but the man who delivered them rarely came across the electronic pulse as the

I remember when I was a little boy, I heard a politician tell a story about a public hanging. The sheriff told the condemned man that under the state law he would be allowed five minutes to choose whatever words he cared to speak as his last act. The prisoner responded, "Mr. Sheriff, I haven't got anything to say, so just get it over with." But a man way in back in the audience jumped up and said, "Well, if he doesn't want those five minutes, Sheriff, I'd like to have them. I'm a candidate for Congress."

# THE JOHNSON WIT

vibrant and captivating person revealed to those who encountered him on a personal basis or in small groups. They were the ones who knew the legendary Johnson the storyteller.

His stories, as one of his assistants said, were not meant for national television. But they had "the color and smell of life." He rarely exercised his wit just to get a laugh. Invariably he used his stories to make a point. And almost always they were rooted in the rich experience of life in the hill country.

Some of the tales he told with relish are presented here.

It's like that preacher with a member of his congregation who always snored through the sermon. He finally got tired of it, and he decided he'd play a little joke on him. While the fellow was sleeping on Sunday, the preacher said in a low voice, "All of you folks that want to go to heaven, please stand." Everybody stood except the snoring fellow in the front row. When they sat down, the preacher said in a very loud voice, "Now all of you folks that want to go to hell, please stand." That stirred the fellow, and when he heard, "Please stand," he jumped up. He looked around and saw that no one else was standing with him and he said, "Preacher, I don't know what it is we're voting on, but you and I seem to be the only two for it."

I was thinking about one of our elder statesmen who found difficulty with his hearing and went to the doctor. The doctor examined him carefully and asked, "How much are you drinking these days?" The fellow said he drank about a pint a day. The doctor said, "Well, if you want to improve your hearing, you are going to have to cut out your drinking." About 90 days later the fellow went back to the doctor and his hearing hadn't improved a bit. "Have you cut out your drinking?" the doctor asked. He said, "No." "Well, I can't do anything for you if won't follow my advice," the doctor said. "Didn't I tell you when you were here that you should cut out your drinking if you wanted to improve your hearing?" He said, "Yes." "Well, why didn't you do it?" the doctor asked. The patient said, "Doctor, I got home and I considered it, and I just decided that I liked what I drank so much better than what I heard."

Someone brought a big black bulldog into the neighborhood, and pretty soon the whole neighborhood was flourishing with little black dogs. Very much to the distress of the ladies of the neighborhood, they had dogs on every porch. They decided to do something about it, and after consulting one of the veterinarians, took the dog down and had him operated on. There was a relative calm in the community for a period of two or three years, and then pretty soon the dogs started flowering again. Puppies were seen waddling down the sidewalks. The ladies were upset. "Well, I'll tell you what's happened," one of them said. "It's that damn black bulldog; that's what's causing it all." "But we had him operated on," another one objected. "I know it," the first one said, "but now he's acting as a consultant."

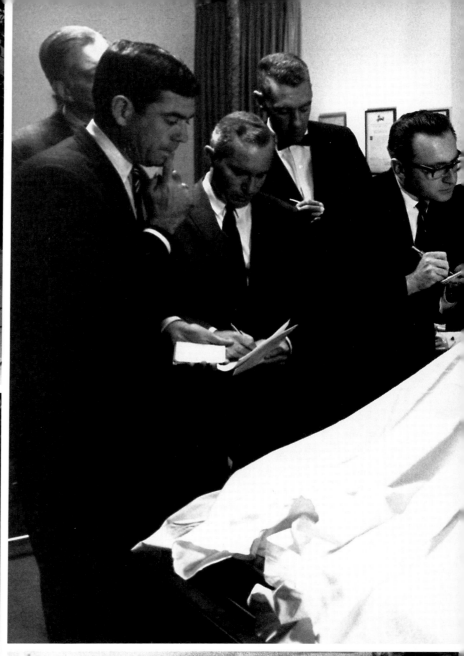

# WORKING METHODS

## HIS OFFICE WAS WHEREVER HE WAS

# THE JOHNSON TREATMENT

# THE PRESS

**N**ear the close of his Administration, Lyndon

Johnson told a reporter: "Our most tragic error may have been our inability to establish a rapport and a

confidence with the communications media. I don't think the press has understood me."

Perhaps his own assessment of his media relations should be taken at face value. After the Vietnam effort

began to decay, some in the news media could find little that was "right" with Johnson. Generally, these

were the same people who backed him wholeheartedly in achieving the great social reforms of 1964–65.

Compared to his successors in the Presidency, however, Johnson may have had better press relations than

he believed. He was always accessible and enjoyed talking with reporters, especially in private. He could

expand on a whole range of issues, calling up from memory more facts and figures than the average person

can assimilate. He could talk about the thing with which he was most familiar: his job. And he would be

discussing it with men and women who understood the issues.

Johnson had four press secretaries during his five years in office, but in many respects he was his own press

secretary. A President so mindful of press coverage and so active in all phases of government could not be

anything but his own negotiator and debater with the news media. Perhaps he bared his breast so often to

the reporters he was bound to receive more wounds than a more reticent leader might receive.

—GEORGE CHRISTIAN

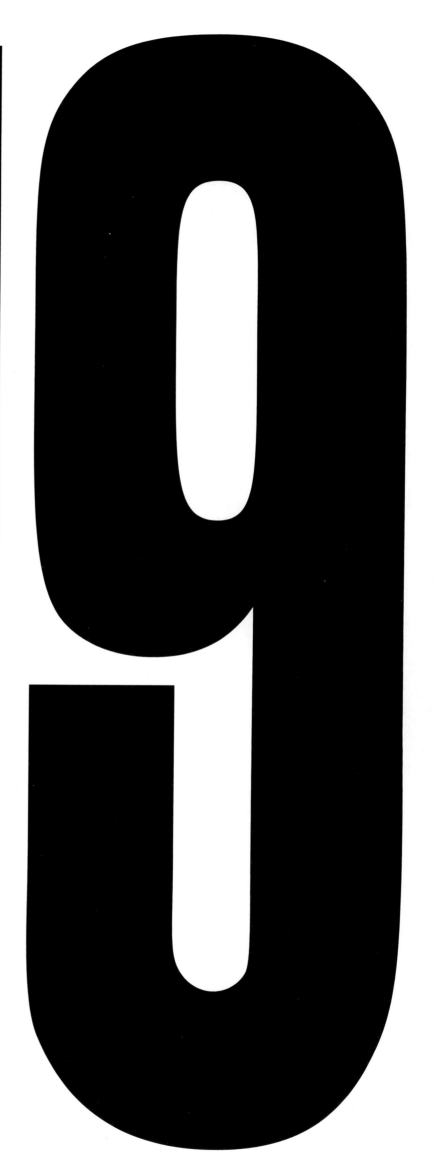

The great adventure of the 1960s—
the space program, in which American astronauts climbed step by step toward
the moon—produced its first tragedy in January. On a day that would otherwise have been remembered for its triumph—a treaty was signed at the White
House to keep weapons of war out of space—Apollo astronauts Virgil Grissom,
Edward White, and Roger Chaffee were killed in a training accident on the
launchpad. Lyndon Johnson had been intimately involved in the space program from the beginning. As Senator, he had shepherded the legislation creating it. As Vice President, he had recommended the moon effort to Kennedy.
Now, as President, he attended the funerals, comforted the widows, and kept
the program on track. He would live to see men reach the moon, but it would
not be in his Administration.

There were other unforeseen crises that year, each of them heralded by what
Lady Bird called "that most dread and frightening sound that can happen in
this house"—the telephone call in the dark, shattering sleep.

In June, the ever-present hostility between Israel and the neighboring Arab
states erupted with gunfire. When Egypt closed the Gulf of Aqaba to Israeli
shipping, violating an agreement made a decade before, Israeli forces moved in
to open the passage. The result was a war that for six harrowing days kept the
world's eyes riveted on the Middle East. Johnson considered the situation more
dangerous than Vietnam. "The Vietnam conflict, tragic and perilous as it was,"
he said later, "was contained, and we were reasonably sure we could keep it
from spreading. Conflict in the Middle East was something else." The major

**A**t the White House America rolls out her red carpet to the world, and the Johnsons' entertaining was like LBJ: big, expansive, inclusive, and sentimental. President Johnson was a generous host who wanted to share the house with all America. Often he would say to a group of guests, "This is your house; Lady Bird and I only have a short-term lease."

For President and Mrs. Johnson, state dinners were an opportunity to introduce their visitors from abroad to some of the best and most interesting parts of America—in entertainment, people, food, and wine.

Backstage, calligraphers worked their artistry on place cards and menus, the chef and his helpers boned pheasants and peeled mountains of asparagus, in the East Room the pas de deux was rehearsed, florists arranged flowers in vermeil bowls, waiters polished crystal and chilled wines, a writer added an anecdote to the President's toast, the social office shuffled the seating chart to make room for an unexpected guest, members of the Marine Band buttoned their red jackets en route to playing "Hail to the Chief," a maid ran the vacuum one last time, candles were lit, schedules were checked and rechecked so the President and his visitor would appear simultaneously on the North Portico for photographers from around the world.

No matter what the occasion, from the arrival of an envelope that reads simply "The White House" in the upper-left-hand corner to the Marine Band's last bars of a popular show tune, a White House entertainment is a page of history.

—BESS ABELL

The President and Mrs. Johnson
host a state dinner for
Emperor Haile Selassie of Ethiopia.
Following White House tradition
for such events, gifts are exchanged
by the heads of state in the
Executive Mansion before descending
the staircase to join their guests.

Briefings—to Congressional, business, labor, and other groups—remain a White House routine. These occasions find Johnson at his persuasive best, even as his support begins to decline.

Ententainment at the LBJ Ranch
is a colorful — and frequent — feature
of the Johnson years. Here,
the President and First Lady
provide ambassadors from Latin
America with a Texas barbecue
and a spectacle of the Old West
by the Texas Fandangle
on the banks of the Pedernales.

**LBJ meets with the presidents of Latin American countries in Uruguay, where, with his encouragement, an agreement is reached to create a Latin American common market in the 1970s — a commitment that would go unfulfilled.**

danger was confrontation between the two superpowers: the U.S. was committed to preserving the integrity of Israel; Egypt and some of the other Arab states had grown increasingly dependent on the Soviet Union. The "hot line"—a communications link between the Kremlin and the White House installed during the Kennedy Administration to provide the leaders of the two countries with immediate contact in crisis—was used for the first time, as Johnson and Aleksei Kosygin, Chairman of the Soviet Union's Council of Ministers, exchanged assurances of their efforts to end the fighting on behalf of their respective clients. At one point a suddenly ominous message from the Kremlin suggested the possibility of Soviet intrusion into the action. Johnson ordered a show of naval strength as a warning that any such move would be resisted. In the White House Situation Room the President and his advisers waited, tense and apprehensive. Then the Kremlin sent a new, more conciliatory message. The crisis passed. A cease-fire was hammered out in the United Nations, and the Six-Day War ended.

Soon thereafter, Johnson and Kosygin met face-to-face, in Glassboro, New Jersey—selected because it was halfway between Washington and New York, where Kosygin was attending a meeting at the United Nations. In the home of Dr. Thomas Robinson, the president of Glassboro State College, they talked about the tensions in the Middle East, the war in Vietnam, and the missile race in which their two countries were engaged.

Then he went off to Texas to visit his new grandson. Luci had given birth a few days before to Patrick Lyndon Nugent. Johnson told his daughter that his

new status of grandfather had given him the right approach to make to Kosygin, also a grandfather. His grandson would soon become known the world over as Lyn, and as his grandfather's constant companion, a regular on the Washington scene.

The Glassboro talks themselves had produced no resolution of any substance —a matter, Johnson confessed, of considerable "disappointment." But the fact that they had been held in cordial circumstances was itself, he thought, an accomplishment, and to the nation he expressed the hope that the meetings had made the world a little less dangerous.

With the successful passage of the civil rights laws of 1964 and 1965, President Johnson would later write, "the long history of Negro-white relations had entered a new and more bewildering stage." Long-dormant hopes had been aroused, but along with the satisfaction they brought, they also served to illuminate the conditions of life for most black Americans, a life of poverty and slums and unemployment in which resentment had long simmered. "Change was on the horizon," Johnson said, "close enough to ignite hope. but far enough away to increase frustration."

In Detroit that August, the frustration and what LBJ called "the countless years of suppressed anger" erupted when police raided an after-hours drinking club and arrested 73 black patrons. The incident triggered a wave of rioting in the city that soon was out of control.

At the request of the governor, Johnson sent in Federal troops, and the White House became virtually a command post. Order was restored only after days of

**Attending the funeral of Germany's former Chancellor Konrad Adenauer, Johnson meets with European leaders, including** (left) **French President Charles de Gaulle and** (above, top) **German Chancellor Kurt Kiesinger and West Berlin Mayor Willy Brandt.**
(above)
**As a gesture of the kind of personal diplomacy he delights in, the President takes along on the trip Father Wunnibald Schneider, pastor of the Catholic church in Stonewall, Texas, so the parish priest can visit his native land.**

(overleaf)
**The President is aware of the antiwar demonstrations that occur regularly outside the White House. One of the few recorded by White House photographers includes Coretta King, wife of Martin Luther King, and Benjamin Spock.**

**Tension between Israel and the Arab states has been mounting for some time. Just days before hostilities begin, the President meets with** (above) **Abba Eban, Israel's Ambassador to the United States and** (opposite) **Ephraim Evron, Israel's Foreign Minister.**

looting and terror and bloodshed. "We have endured a week such as no nation should live through," the President said when it was over, "a time of violence and tragedy." The phrase "long, hot summer" entered the nation's vocabulary.

Justice Tom Clark, knowing the President wanted to appoint his son, Ramsey Clark, Attorney General, left his seat on the Supreme Court so there would be no appearance of impropriety. Johnson filled the vacancy with Thurgood Marshall, the grandson of a slave, who had been serving as Solicitor General. "It is the right thing to do," said the President, "the right time to do it, the right man and the right place."

In retrospect, mid-1967 appears as the high point of Administration confidence toward the progress of the war in Vietnam. At the beginning of the year, everyone around the President thought all the signs showed the tide was turning. "We are very sure we are on the right track," Johnson himself declared. General Westmoreland was brought home for consultations in March and was invited to address the Congress. His message also was one of assurance. "We will prevail in Vietnam," he told the legislators.

McNamara went over in July and came back optimistic. He dismissed the suggestion, found in many of the media reports from Vietnam, that the fighting was "stalemated," and when the President asked him, "Are we going to be able to win this goddamned war?" he responded, "I am convinced we can achieve our goals and end the fighting if we follow the course we have set for ourselves." U.S. strength there now stood at 463,000 men, and McNamara, Westmoreland, and General Earle Wheeler, Chairman of the Joint Chiefs of Staff, all agreed that it should be increased to 525,000 by the next June.

The reasons for optimism seemed solid enough. Two years before, a Communist takeover of South Vietnam had appeared imminent. That conquest had been averted, and the combined North Vietnamese–Viet Cong forces had yet to win a major battle against the Americans. Moreover, elections had been held in South Vietnam—from which Thieu emerged as President and Ky as Vice President. Johnson invited a team of distinguished Americans to observe the

(following pages)

**Early in the morning of June 5 war does break out in the Middle East, and only a few hours after being awakened with that news, the President is told that, for the first time since it was installed, the "hot line" to Moscow has been activated, and a world crisis of unimagined proportions is imminent. Over the next week, whether in the Oval Office, in the Situation Room, on television, in the Cabinet Room, or in anterooms where aides spend the night, the President and his advisers watch, wait, and try to prevent the Six-Day War from becoming an East-West confrontation. In Washington, the passions aroused by the conflict spill over into the streets.**

Thurgood Marshall
uses the phone
in the Oval Office
to tell his wife
that the President
is nominating him
to the Supreme Court—
the first black to
join that body.
LBJ, wanting the press
to get no inkling of
the appointment until he
can announce it,
tells Marshall to come not
through the usual entrance
where the reporters
might spot him, but through
the one on the other side
of the building
with the tourists,
where he was met.

The eyes of the world focus on
Glassboro, New Jersey, when
the President meets there
with Chairman Aleksei Kosygin
of the Soviet Union.
The atmosphere is cordial,
but no firm agreements result.

**I**f there was a phone call

for him and there wasn't a phone beside wherever

he was sitting, he'd say, "Have one put in."

—MARIE FEHMER

**The President flies to Texas to meet his new grandson, Patrick Lyndon Nugent.**

election. On their return they reported that the election had been an open and free one in which the voters had defied the threat of Communist punishment. The election and the adoption of a constitution persuaded Johnson and his advisers that the foundations for a stable and representative government were being laid in South Vietnam.

Working against this heartening evidence, however, was the growing realization that despite enormous losses the Communists showed no signs of flagging. They seemed to be at least as strong as they had been a year before. Ellsworth Bunker, U.S. Ambassador in Saigon, reported: "Hanoi seems determined to continue the war in anticipation that we will get tired of the heavy burdens we are carrying."

It was under this ominous and gathering awareness—that the enemy was prepared to endure everything and still outlast the United States—that the Administration's solid front began to erode. By September, the optimistic

Camp David, a retreat in Maryland's Catoctin Mountains,
named by President Eisenhower for his grandson,
is intended as a place where Presidents can enjoy privacy
and escape the pressures of the White House. On this June
weekend, the retreat is filled with aides and friends,
and White House photographers are given the rare
opportunity of recording the house and grounds.

McNamara of July was warning about the ineffectiveness of the bombing, and in October he became a critic of the policy he had helped to create. "The continuation of our present course of action in Southeast Asia," he told the President, "would be dangerous, costly in lives, and unsatisfactory to the American people."

With the war now costing $70 million a day, Johnson asked Congress for legislation imposing a 10 percent surcharge on corporate and individual income taxes, warning of the "spiral of ruinous inflation" that would come without it. But the proposal was decisively shelved in committee. There was a restlessness in the Congress now, not so much rebellion as uneasiness, "a growing feeling," as one journal put it, "that somehow the United States should be accomplishing more with the men it now has in Vietnam."

That uneasiness mirrored the mood of the country in general, a mood fed not only by the staggering costs but even more by the sobering casualty figures: more than 12,000 American men had now been killed in that distant land.

Disaffection was accelerating rapidly. Robert Kennedy, who had been moving toward an open break with the President, confirmed it with a speech on the Senate floor. Other Senators began making their opposition known. A full week of antiwar demonstrations included a massive march on the Pentagon, and the newspapers of the world were filled with pictures of young men and women inserting flowers into the barrels of rifles held by soldiers keeping them at bay. But it wasn't just the young on the streets anymore. Their demonstrations were joined now by businessmen and housewives.

A new subculture born with the antiwar movement had suddenly become part of the national scene: the hippies. Curious about them, the President was driven one Sunday around Dupont Circle, which he had been told was their Washington gathering place. He circled the area twice, looking out his window at the ragged scene that was fast becoming part of the American image, and returned in silence to the White House.

He went on a swing of military bases and an aircraft carrier in the Pacific. He ended his trip in Williamsburg, Virginia, where he attended Sunday church services and heard the rector say from the pulpit, "There is a rather general consensus that what we are doing in Vietnam is wrong."

In a speech in San Antonio, Johnson went a step further toward conciliation than he had before. He had always asked for some signal from the Communists that they were willing to wind down the war before he would ground his bombers. Now, in what became known as the "San Antonio formula," he offered to stop bombing and negotiate with no advance gestures from either side.

But nothing seemed to work, either in Hanoi or in his own country. For the first time, a majority of the people polled said they were against his handling of the war. His own popularity, which had risen for a while after Glassboro, dropped to below 40 percent. Johnson himself ruefully observed that he might wind up with the approval of only 1 percent of the people.

He was becoming more and more identified in the public mind with the war. But with his once massive support declining, the unanimity within his Administration cracking, the nation troubled with doubts and dissension, Johnson showed no signs of changing course. "Waist deep in the Big Muddy, and the old fool says to push on," went a protest song of the times. Some later writers would also offer up the image of a stubborn and bullish leader blindly plowing toward disaster because he could not admit the bankruptcy of his policy, or because he was determined to bend history to his will, no matter the cost.

But the image is at considerable variance with other perceptions and realities. One veteran of the protest movement, who carried his dislike for Johnson into his own middle age, articulated an inconsistency that bothered many Johnson foes: "A guy like that, who always knew how to look out for his own interests, wouldn't have let the war drag him down. He would have found a

**Riots erupt in Detroit's black neighborhoods, and the White House becomes a command post as the President sends in Federal troops to restore order. Johnson appoints a blue-ribbon commission, chaired by Illinois Governor Otto Kerner, to study the causes of violence in America, and he addresses the nation in an effort to restore calm.**

LIVE THROUGH
A TIME OF
VIOLENCE AND
TRAGEDY.
FOR A FEW
MINUTES TONIGHT
I WANT TO TALK
ABOUT

Among the President's visitors this
fall are (top) **cellist Pablo Casals**,
(right) **Soviet Ambassador Anatoly Dobrynin**,
**and children whom the President greets in the**
**Oval Office** (above) **and Mrs. Johnson and Vice**
**President Humphrey entertain at a White**
**House fair** (opposite).

(following pages)
**The Commander in Chief makes a Veterans**
**Day visit to the aircraft carrier** *Enterprise*.

**At Williamsburg, Virginia, the President attends a church service and hears the rector criticize U.S. policy in Vietnam.**

way to cut out long before that to save his ass. I'm no fan of the guy, but you can't have it both ways."

Nor does the image square with the Lyndon Johnson who subordinated all his traits, including stubbornness, to a lifetime mastery of the art of compromise.

Why, then, did he stay on the road that had led to this difficult hour?

The answer of those around him at the time, those who knew him best, leads back to the Johnson Bill Moyers saw in those troubled days when he made his fateful decision for limited war. He knew the cost, as he had in the beginning, to him and his Presidency. But he believed still, as he had then, that he had no other course: bad as the war was, the alternative was a surrender that would lead to worse. And for a while yet, he would still hope that the American people would see again the danger as he did.

But he could not get through to them.

There was a moment when it seemed that he might. George Christian, his press secretary, set up a televised press conference in which the President's words were carried through a miniature microphone hung around his neck rather than from the usual one attached to a podium. Suddenly freed of the podium's restraints, the stiff and formal Johnson seemed to disappear, and there instead was the Lyndon Johnson of the courthouse steps working his magic on the crowd—folksy, friendly, persuasive, and convincing.

He was showered with messages of congratulations from his staff, his friends, and the people of Boise and Pittsburgh and Jackson who had been turning him off for so long.

It was a stunning success—and it was never repeated. He was worried that he had not been sufficiently "Presidential."

In December, the Johnsons' older daughter, Lynda Bird, captured the nation's attention by marrying Marine Captain Charles Robb in a glittering White House wedding.

And then the President went around the world. Australian Prime Minister Harold Holt, one of his staunchest allies, had drowned. Johnson went to Melbourne for the memorial service. While he was there he met with the Australian cabinet. He told them he knew the Communists were planning a major offensive in Vietnam, and he repeated his determination to stand firm. He went to Cam Ranh Bay for another visit with the troops, who raised their voices in cheers when he arrived. He spoke to them with feeling, telling them what they were doing for their country was important, and that, despite the protests they had been hearing about, their nation loved them. They listened with respect and cheered him again when he left. He did not go home from there but on to Rome, where all along he had secretly planned a meeting with the Pope.

It was Christmas Eve in Vatican City as he and Paul VI exchanged their greetings and their hopes that each could find a way to peace.

**LBJ confers with General Westmoreland, whom he has called home from Vietnam for consultations.**

LBJ's aides have long
wanted to see him
come across on
television as he does
with small groups.
At one televised press
conference, freed of the
podium by virtue
of a small microphone
around his neck,
he is able to act
as the vintage Johnson
the public rarely sees.
Aides are delighted,
but he never repeats
the performance, fearing
it is not sufficiently
"Presidential."

**M**y last night as a single lady had been a cacophony of memories—sad and happy. At the end of the rehearsal dinner, Daddy took Chuck aside and told him that we had a problem: The private plane we were chartering to get away on our honeymoon belonged to a company that, unknown to us, was going to be bought by a larger company that had government contracts, so it would be embarrassing to Daddy if we used it. There we were with no way to get to our honeymoon spot, and no place to spend our wedding night. The woes of politics.

There are many poignant memories of my great day. All the bridesmaids in long hair—some with falls to mask their own short hair—in their brilliant Geoffrey Beene red dresses, gave a regal appearance to the ceremony. Mother had been reluctant to dress the bridesmaids in red, but I persuaded her that it would not mark them as "scarlet women" but simply as wearing "Robb red." As I waited at the top of the stairs, Mr. Beene straightened my heavy white gown for the last time. I could see the sadness in Daddy's eyes.

The ceremony itself was a circus—hundreds of friends, including a few former beaux, standing in the Great Hall and East Room peering for a view; my Aunt Rebekah regal at almost six feet tall with a hat that reached to Olympus; the altar where we had forgotten to light the candles—and behind the altar, tiny Bonnie Angelo, a pool reporter.

My regrets—there were so many people from so far away whom I only glimpsed or said a quick word to in the receiving line. My dress was so heavy that my shoulders ached, and I was relieved after two hours when the receiving line was over.

As a final, nostalgic moment, Chuck and I gave each of our parents a crystal-topped shadow box encasing our symbols: a gold bulldog for Chuck's Marines and a gold bird with an arrow through the heart, which was also the pin I gave my bridesmaids. Then Daddy flew off to Texas with a planeload of friends and family—and Chuck and I were alone (with the Secret Service) to celebrate our honeymoon.

—LYNDA JOHNSON ROBB

The death of Australian
Prime Minister
Harold Holt stimulates
a five-day
round-the-world trip:
first to the memorial
service in
Melbourne; then to
Vietnam to confer
with Westmoreland;
on to an air base
in Thailand to visit
with U.S. pilots;
a stop in Pakistan
for a hurried
conference with
President Ayub Khan;
to Vatican City
and a meeting with
the Pope; then
finally home
for Christmas.

BRANCH

LADY
BIRD

**A**s the wife of an increasingly important member of the government establishment, Lady Bird Johnson had been part of the Washington scene for 30 years. But like her husband, she was not well known to the nation at large when she became First Lady.

Christened Claudia when she was born in 1912, she had been given in infancy the nickname that stuck through life. After her mother's death when she was 5, she was raised in the small east Texas town of Karnack by her father, a moderately prosperous landowner and proprietor of a general store ("T. J. Taylor—Dealer in Everything," the sign over his building read), and a maiden aunt. "I grew up rather alone," she recalled. "My brothers were older and off at school. There weren't any playmates my age."

It was in this rural and solitary atmosphere that she began to experience the kinship with nature that later would be demonstrated on a national scale. She was, as her husband once described her, "a shy girl who liked to roam the forest." She remembered how she "ran unhampered down the sandy roads and hedgerows, finding dewberries and blackberries and pink climbing roses, and explored the piney woods near my house. The song of the wind in the upper branches of the pine trees was the most evocative symphony I've ever heard."

She studied history in college, and trained to be a journalist. But marriage to Lyndon Johnson after a whirlwind courtship set her on another course. (Reflecting on their first date, she said: "I knew I had met something remarkable, but I didn't quite know what.") He was then secretary—a job later known as "administrative assistant"—to Congressman Richard Kleberg in Washington, but they moved to Texas a few months later when President Roosevelt appointed him state director of the National Youth Administration.

When the opportunity presented itself for LBJ to make a run for Congress in a special election in 1937, Lady Bird used part of her inheritance from her mother to help finance his successful campaign. (She used the rest of it later to acquire the Austin radio station that became the nucleus of the family business, and eventually the source of its fortune.)

She managed his Congressional office while he was overseas with the Navy in World War II, was a gracious hostess during his Senate years as she was rearing two daughters, nursed him back to health after his massive heart attack in 1955, traveled with him when he was Vice President—and on those journeys made a host of admirers overseas. Those who knew her agreed with Sam Rayburn: "The smartest thing Lyndon ever did was to marry her."

The nation at large first saw her on that dark night at an air base outside Washington when Air Force One landed with the body of John Kennedy, and the new President stepped to the microphone solemnly to utter his first words to a shaken people. "There she was," wrote a Washington reporter, "at his side, as she had always been."

Thrust into the glare of public attention, she said, "I feel as if I'm suddenly on stage for a part I never rehearsed," but she moved through the part sure-footedly, sounding all the right grace notes. She stopped speculation about when the bereaved Jacqueline Kennedy would move out of the White House and the Johnsons move in with the statement: "I would to God I could serve

Mrs. Kennedy's comfort. I can at least serve her convenience." To the country learning about her, she came across as sincere, real, natural, composed—"a lady of exceptional grace," the Washington *Post* put it.

She made it clear that she saw that her first duty was to be her husband's helpmate, looking out for his comfort and welfare—"custodian of the President himself," *Newsweek* observed, and then added: "...so far as that headstrong man would ever countenance one."

It was precisely that dimension of their relationship—her calm against his volatility—that elicited the most interest. She had long since adjusted to his erratic and demanding habits and had described him as "an exciting man to live with; an exhausting man to keep up with; a man who has worn well in the years we have been together, and whom I want to spend the rest of my life with." Liz Carpenter, who had known them since the early Forties and served as the First Lady's staff director, once described them in theatrical terms: "He was the star at center stage. She was in charge of the props and always part of the whole performance."

He confided in her with complete trust. When asked for them, she contributed ideas for the President's speeches. Asked or not, she monitored those speeches, grading him on both content and delivery. Whenever she passed him a note telling him he had talked too long, he would bring his address to a close and sit down—sometimes first calling attention to the warning she had given him. "He accords me the very fine compliment," she said, "of thinking I have good judgment." James Rowe, a friend from early New Deal days together, said, "she had far more influence on him than anyone ever knew."

But custodian though she was, she was also a concerned and intelligent woman who wanted, as she later acknowledged, "to serve my husband *and* serve the country," and who saw her position as a platform that could be used.

She traveled to the depressed areas of Kentucky and Pennsylvania where the first battles of the war on poverty would be fought—"to see the flesh and blood behind the statistics." She went to Greece to represent the President at King Paul's funeral, and she visited the space center in Alabama (where she spoke of "the staggering potential this project has for all mankind"). At the White House, she continued the tradition of state dinners for visiting dignitaries, named the East Garden for Jacqueline Kennedy, and formalized her predecessor's effort to ensure the historic integrity of the Mansion with the Committee for the Preservation of the White House. She initiated a series of "women do-ers" luncheons, highlighting for the press women who were making a contribution in their various fields. She officiated at ceremonies swearing in naturalized citizens. She foreshadowed the new age of women's involvement by telling the graduating females of Radcliffe College: "The world cries out for your participation from Appalachia's one-room schools to the cement jungles of our cities" and challenging them to try to "achieve the precious balance between women's domestic and civil life."

The *U.S. News and World Report*, summing it all up at the end of the new Administration's first half-year, reported: "Lady Bird Johnson is setting a pace as First Lady that hasn't been matched since Eleanor Roosevelt's day." Comparisons with Mrs. Roosevelt were coming frequently. Lady Bird's reaction was, "Mrs. Roosevelt was a very great human being. I'd like to be as good as she was. I have no feeling that I am."

Others did. "You're doing a wonderful job," Robert Kennedy told her after only a few months. "Everybody says so." And in fact, "everybody" *was* saying as much. One columnist cited friends forecasting that "she will one day take her place as one of America's great First Ladies." Said *Newsweek,* she is "showing the promise of being one of the most notable—and vital—First Ladies in the history of the Presidency."

Asked what "image" she would like to create, she replied, "My image will emerge in deeds, not in words."

The image that was to be her particular and unique identification came together bit by bit during that first year in the White House. Looking out of her plane window on her early trip to Appalachia, she recorded in her diary impressions that signaled the cause she would ultimately embrace as her own: "When you saw the vast scars across the landscape from the mining…you couldn't help from thinking that God has done his best by this country, but man has certainly done his worst, and now it is up to man to repair the damage." The references to the nation's natural beauty in the President's commencement address at the University of Michigan were the parts of the speech that made her "heart sing," she said. "That was sort of the beginning…It was right down my alley because nature had given me so much joy and serenity and good days and happy memories…" She was learning that "I had the opportunity to do more than just enjoy the beauty I had experienced over the years. I took advantage of the public stage it provided…"

She started with Washington, "simply because that's where we lived. You begin where you are." Buoyed by her husband's admiring support, she formed a committee of prestigious citizens to help develop "A More Beautiful National Capital." Flowers and trees and shrubs were planted everywhere. The public parks and monumental spaces of official Washington were transformed so that each spring they would burst into color anew. Another kind of transformation was attempted—with less dramatic results but lasting effects—in the inner city, with the creation of playgrounds and oases of flowers and grass.

In a number of ways the effort spread across the country—known, she lamented, "by the unimaginative name of beautification," which "sounds purely cosmetic." "Alas," she said later, "we never did think of a better word." The search for a "better word" constantly troubled her as she was applying it to specific—and varied—projects. She encouraged citizens in every community to spruce up their neighborhoods, prodded merchants and filling station owners to plant and grow and paint. She was the moving force behind the Highway Beautification Act of 1965, which was designed to remove the billboards and junkyards that obscured the traveler's view of the countryside. Trailed by a train of reporters, she floated by raft down the Rio Grande, explored the redwood forest, and camped out in national parks to acquaint her countrymen with the glories of their native land.

But even these could not contain the meaning of "beautification." It came to represent the entire subject of the environment, and more. "Tackling the subject of beautification," she recorded at the time, "is like picking up a tangled skein of wool—all the threads are interwoven: public plantings…clean air… clean water…highway beautification…the protection of our parklands and seashores. It is hard to hitch the conversation into one straight line, because everything leads to something else."

It was a "tangled skein" of the greatest importance, for it brought together a leader and a cause at the right historic moment. For more than any other factor, it was the effort led by a First Lady that made the country conscious of the gathering threat to its native splendor and its natural resources.

She declined credit for doing anything more than "walking it on stage." But Americans knew better. "Lady Bird Johnson," wrote historian Lewis Gould, "[took] the amorphous and ill-defined possibilities of the institution of First Lady and…stretched them into a significant campaign for an important national priority. The little girl on Caddo Lake had come far from the flowers and fields of East Texas…When her opportunity came to be an advocate for the preservation and perpetuation of the nation's environment, she seized it with dedication, commitment, and lasting results. She fulfilled her obligation 'to keep the beauty of the landscape as we remember it…and to leave [it] for our grandchildren.' She had also amply paid her rent for the space that she had occupied in the world, and she had enriched the history of the United States with her presence."

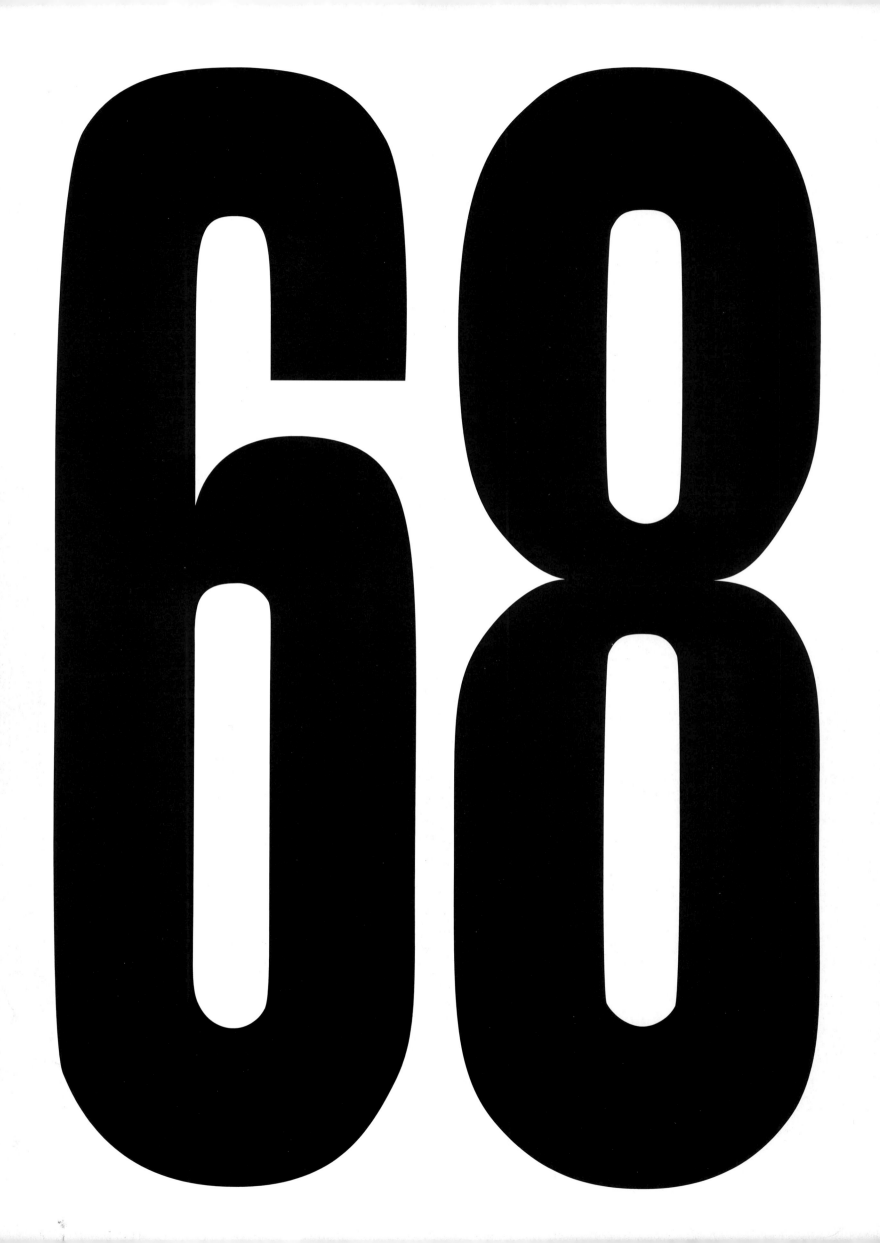

Protest reaches inside the White House when entertainer Eartha Kitt attacks the war at a luncheon given by Mrs. Johnson for "women do-ers." She confronts the President, on his brief visit to the group, with a question about child care.

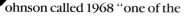

**J**ohnson called 1968 "one of the most agonizing years any President ever spent in the White House. I sometimes felt that I was living in a continuous nightmare." It was also the year he changed course on Vietnam and forfeited his chance for a second full term in the Presidency.

He did not relinquish his belief that he and his advisers were following the right path in Vietnam. But the difference now was his realization that he could no longer hope to rally the nation to follow him on that path. As Dean Rusk later recalled, "people at the grass roots, quite apart from those campus demonstrators and people like that, had finally decided that if we couldn't tell them when the war was going to be over, we'd better chuck it. President Johnson felt that people at the grass roots had decided we ought to get out of Vietnam."

The denouement began at the end of January, on the new year holiday known to the Vietnamese as Tet, with a coordinated attack by the Communists against most of the major cities and military installations in South Vietnam.

The assaults were quickly beaten back, most of them in just a few days, by U.S. and South Vietnamese troops. Despite their massive commitment of forces, and the heavy losses they took in the attack, the Communists were not able either to hold the cities or to encourage an uprising by the people inside them. They did not crack or cripple South Vietnam's army. In short, none of their objectives was accomplished. In the streets and the countryside of Vietnam, the assault was a military failure.

The war enters a new phase when Communist forces mount their Tet Offensive against cities in the South. Although they do not achieve their objectives, the strength of their effort rocks the United States, and public disaffection grows rapidly.
(overleaf)
A beleaguered President says farewell to troops returning to Vietnam for a second tour.

*Tonight I want to speak to you of peace in Vietnam and Southeast Asia.*

*No other question so preoccupies our people...*

*In the hope that this action will lead to early talks, I am taking the first step to de-escalate the conflict. We are reducing —substantially reducing—the present level of hostilities.*

*And we are doing so unilaterally, and at once...*

*With America's sons in the fields far away, with America's future under challenge right here at home, with our hopes and the world's hopes for peace in the balance every day, I do not believe that I should devote an hour or a day of my time to any personal partisan causes or to any duties other than the awesome duties of this office—the Presidency of our country.*

*Accordingly, I shall not seek, and I will not accept, the nomination of my party for another term as your President.*

Address to the Nation
March 31, 1968

**LBJ couples an announcement of the de-escalation of the war with the stunning declaration that he will not seek another term.** (top right) **Lady Bird coaches him on how to pace his televised address to the nation.** (opposite and middle right) **After the address, he watches a playback of the speech, accompanied by a tearful Luci.** (bottom right) **At day's end, the President and Mrs. Johnson take the calls of friends and well-wishers.**

**S**enator Kennedy's wire to President Johnson following the President's withdrawal statement on Sunday [March 31] included a request for a meeting to which President Johnson on Monday agreed in a public statement…

We were escorted to the Cabinet Room and were told the meeting was to be held there with us sitting across from the President, who was to have two aides present, Walt Rostow and Charlie Murphy. I whispered that it sounded as though the Indian Treaty Room would be more appropriate. The President, looking extremely fit, came in carrying his grandson, addressed RFK as "Senator," showed us that his grandson could walk at 8 months, sat down, and showed us the dispatch from Hanoi radio regarding possible peace talks. Of the approximately one hour and forty minutes that followed, a majority of the time was spent on Vietnam…

The entire conversation was frank but conciliatory. The President did 90 percent of the talking, referred to the ill feeling between them and to the Senator's attacks on his policy, and stated that he had removed himself from the Presidential contest to prevent his bid from being politically suspect by those groups whom he seemed unable to win: the Kennedy and McCarthy followers and three groups for whom he had accomplished a lot—students, Negroes, and academics. RFK expressed regret for the gap in their relations and *acknowledged his share of the blame. By the end of the conversation the President had mellowed even more, regretting that he had permitted relations to deteriorate...*

*RFK then requested a discussion of the President's role in the forthcoming campaign. LBJ said he felt close to Hubert Humphrey, who had been loyal in a job which no man had ever liked—"and you wouldn't have liked it either," he said to RFK—but he expounded at some length on his present attitude of neutrality and nonparticipation. He added that he was not foreclosing his right to support someone later on...*

*LBJ stressed that he had always felt he was carrying on the Kennedy-Johnson partnership begun in 1960, that he had resisted the suggestion of John Connally and others that all Kennedy people should be replaced, and that he hoped when his service was finished JFK looking down would feel he had faithfully carried on the partnership in the interest of the stockholders. He said Humphrey had not yet discussed the Presidency with him nor had he discussed it with Democratic leaders since his announcement...*

*The atmosphere became increasingly warm and friendly throughout. At one point, in response to the President's restating his self-denial of political ambitions in order to obtain peace, RFK said, "You are a brave and dedicated man"...RFK requested the President see him or at least inform him before altering his position of neutrality. The President agreed to this but acknowledged the possibility of making a non-neutral statement if angered. We parted with expressions of appreciation and friendship on all sides, having gone some 40 minutes overtime. A friendly Secret Service man informed us that Humphrey was the next visitor...*

—THEODORE C. SORENSEN
From his notes on a meeting with the President,
April 3, 1968

**The President learns, via news ticker, that in response to his address, North Vietnam is willing to negotiate.**

But in the newsrooms and boardrooms and main streets of America, the Tet Offensive, as it would be known to history, achieved a victory richer than battlefield triumph: the final collapse of popular support for an unpopular war. The fact that the enemy could even muster the strength for such an assault, the discovery that Communist troops had actually gotten inside the compound housing the American Embassy, the horrifying photograph of the chief of the South Vietnamese national police firing his pistol against the head of a captured Communist—the whole bewildering jumble of images and information about a cause gone awry triggered massive disillusionment. "What's going on here?"

the veteran and popular newscaster Walter Cronkite exploded. "I thought we were winning this war." "If I've lost Cronkite," Johnson told George Christian, "I've lost the country."

As the year began, there was peril from an unexpected source as well. In the international waters off the coast of Communist North Korea, the unarmed U.S. intelligence ship *Pueblo* was seized by the North Koreans. One crew member was killed and the rest taken prisoner. The reasons for the North Korean action baffled the Administration, although after the Tet Offensive there was speculation that the two incidents were related. Americans were

**Vice President Humphrey confers with the Chief Executive shortly after the March 31 speech.**

Spring becomes a season of
shocks that scar the nation.
"Sometimes," Lady Bird records
in her diary, "it seems
the bravest act is just to get up
in the morning." Martin Luther King
is assassinated in Memphis,
touching off riots in cities
across the country.
(left) With Joe Califano,
the President charts
the outbreaks in Washington
and (right) then takes to the air
to see the damage for himself.
(below) He calls on black leaders
to help restore calm.

(overleaf)
Hardly has this siege of violence
ended when Robert Kennedy
is shot to death in Los Angeles.
The President calls his
condolences to
the Kennedy family
as the First Lady looks on.

In Honolulu, LBJ meets for the last time
with Nguyen Van Thieu, now South Vietnam's President.
Thieu's confidence, Johnson would later remark,
never seemed greater.

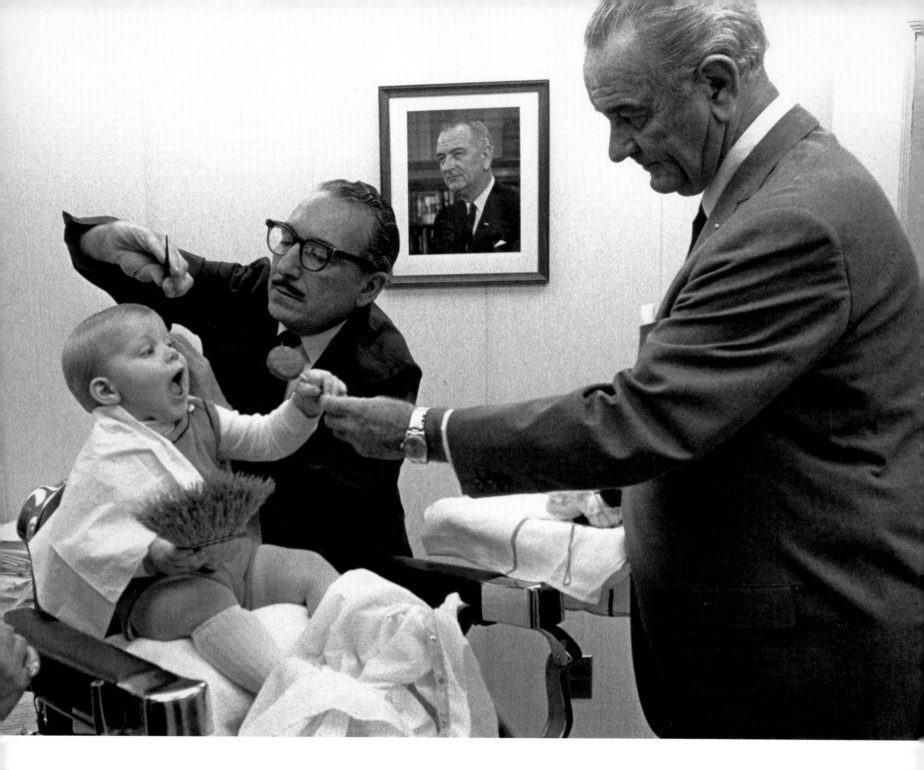

outraged, and now the pressures on the President were for some kind of direct action that would express that anger. But holding the safe return of the crew as the objective, he decided to pursue every avenue of diplomacy rather than any of the military options presented. For the eleven months the North Koreans held the ship and crew before releasing them, the experience would be a constant and tormenting frustration to an increasingly beleaguered President.

For months, Johnson had been worrying about whether to run for a second term in 1968. Throughout 1967 he had talked about it increasingly to family members, close friends, and associates. Some of them did not take him seriously. One who did was his wife, who knew well the source and the anguish of his dilemma. "What weighs heaviest on Lyndon's mind," she confided to her diary, "is: Can he unite the country?" Early in the year she recorded: "His mind is lashed to the inescapable problem of 'How and when do I face up to running again or getting out?'…He keeps looking from one to the other of us for an answer. There is nobody who can decide but him."

In February, Senator Eugene McCarthy, who had announced late in 1967 that he would oppose Johnson for the Democratic nomination, won 42 percent of the party's vote in the New Hampshire primary—a proportion so much higher than expected that it was considered a victory. (Although not on the ticket, LBJ received 49 percent of the vote through write-ins.) And because McCarthy was

**Grandson Lyn is a source of constant pleasure to the President and a menace to the White House telephone system, having inherited his grandfather's obsession with that instrument.**

**A new character is added to the group of LBJ's favorite companions—a dog named Yuki.**

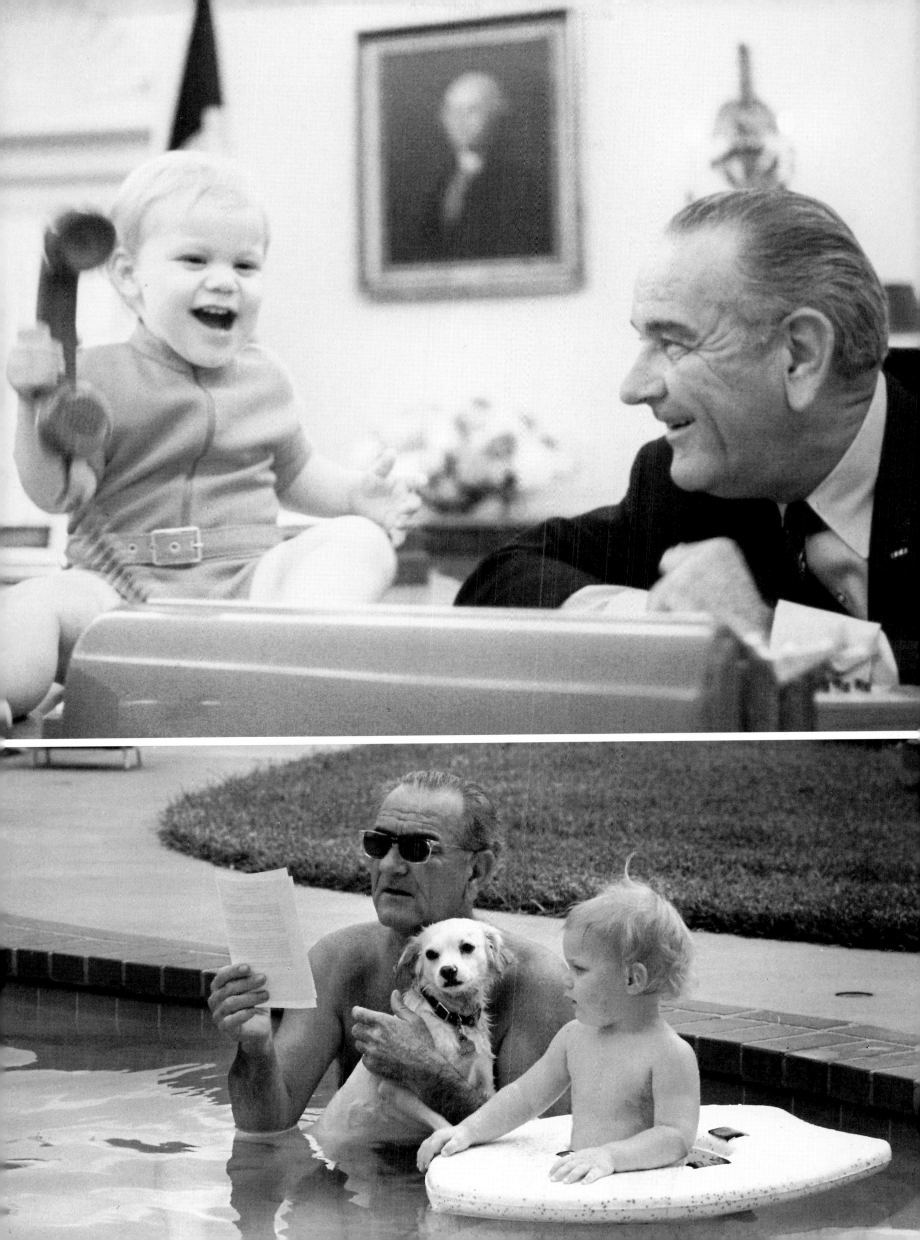

**M**y husband had never in his whole life come home for lunch, and now—well, the Mansion and the office are connected by corridors. We prepared what he wanted so he could keep right on working, bringing staff members or guests. He was at home more and we did more things together.

This life could be very hard on the children. But I did think the opportunities far outweighed the strain, so I wanted to expose them to all the opportunities, but you couldn't buffer them from the strain. If they've got ears, they're going to hear that shouting outside the window protesting the war in Vietnam. That was very painful, particularly in the last year, when each of them had a husband over there. But they also got to see this great country in a marvelous way. They met a lot of people and had a lot of doors opened to them that wouldn't have been otherwise. It was an expanding experience.

So you would have to be a clod, unfeeling, unseeing, not to enjoy being in that position. You also suffered, but in reality you're a more complete human being if you can have both joy and suffering. And you sure didn't have boredom.

I wouldn't trade anything for the experience. But not for anything would I pay the price of admission again.

—LADY BIRD JOHNSON

Richard Nixon, winner of the Republican
nomination for President, confers
about the job with the man he hopes to replace.

THE UNFINISHED AGENDA

THE MAJOR UNFINISHED BUSINESS OF THE 90th CONGRESS INCLUDES:

- HIGHER EDUCATION ACT AMENDMENTS, INCLUDING EDUCATION FOR THE PUBLIC SERVICE, EDUCATION-AL OPPORTUNITY ACT, NETWORKS FOR KNOWLEDGE, EXTENSION OF HIGHER EDUCATION ACT (Conference)

- PARTNERSHIP FOR LEARNING AND EARNING (Conference)

- PIPELINE SAFETY (Conference report adopted by House)

- WHOLESOME POULTRY ACT (Conference)

- NATIONAL WATER COMMISSION (Conference)

- SCENIC TRAILS (Conference)

- CENTRAL ARIZONA PROJECT (Conference)

- HEALTH SERVICES AMENDMENTS, INCLUDING ALCOHOLIC AND NARCOTIC REHABILITATION, MIGRANT HEALTH, REGIONAL MEDICAL PROGRAM, AND SOLID WASTE DISPOSAL (Conference)

- VETERA...        Y (Conference)

a dove, it was considered a dove's victory. Subsequent research would show that much of McCarthy's strength had in fact come from disenchanted hawks looking for a way to register their opposition to Johnson's middle-of-the-road policy. No matter. What the vote revealed was what the President had feared: a split so deep that unity under him would be extremely difficult to achieve.

"A President," Johnson had said on other occasions, "is the instrument of the will of the people." And now, in what Clark Clifford, who had succeeded McNamara as Secretary of Defense, described as "the most painful process you ever saw a man go through," he made the decision to do what he heard the people say to do: wind down the war. And the decision gave him what he called "the right forum" from which to make known his other decision. On March 31 he went before the nation on television. He announced that he was taking the first step to de-escalate the conflict by ordering aircraft and naval vessels to halt their attacks on most of North Vietnam. Then, to certify the sincerity of his effort, he removed himself and his political fortunes from the picture: "I shall not seek—and will not accept—the nomination of my party for another term as your President."

**As the year draws closer to an end, the President is acutely conscious of what he terms the "unfinished agenda." It prompts him to repeat many times, to the delight of his audiences but often the dismay of his staff, a story about Winston Churchill being visited during World War II by ladies of the British Temperance Union. The leader of the group confronted him with the charge that all the brandy he had drunk in the course of the war would half fill the room they were in. Looking at the halfway mark, the Prime Minister said wistfully, "So little have we done," and then, casting his eyes to the ceiling: "So much we have yet to do."**

I was elected to the Texas state senate in November 1966 and started serving my first term in January 1967. It was a given that I would be ignored by the governor of Texas since I was the first black female state senator in this state. But I got a telegram when I was in the senate that said, "You are invited to meet with me on a given date in the Oval Office at the White House. Present this telegram at the East Gate of the West Wing and enter." It was signed by the President...I went into the senate chamber that next day, and I said, "Well, the governor of Texas does not know that I am in the senate, but the President of the United States knows it."

I went to that meeting at the White House. He wanted to talk about the 1968 Housing Act, and we were in the Cabinet Room seated around the table. I said to myself, "He's got civil rights leaders—Whitney Young, people like that, and he doesn't know why I'm here, I'm sure." But Lyndon Johnson never did anything by accident, and as he got into his agenda and finished what he had to say and listened to various people, then he turned his head sharply and said, "Barbara, what do you think about this?" And the next day, do you know what happened? An article in the Evans and Novak column said, "The star at the White House was Barbara Jordan!" You and I know it was an obvious plant, but so what? I was the beneficiary. I just want you to get some sense of how genuinely Lyndon Johnson cared about black people. He cared about all people, but he had a really special thing when it came to black people.

Lyndon Johnson is and was Mr. Civil Rights...

—BARBARA JORDAN

The fateful words had been drafted only that morning with the help of Horace Busby, who had worked on and off for Johnson through the years. Aware of LBJ's penchant for keeping his options open, Busby was not entirely convinced that he would actually say them, and Johnson himself later acknowledged: "Up until the last minute I could have decided not to use the statement. But I can't imagine anything that would have stopped me, unless they accused Lady Bird of stealing the dome off the Capitol, or Westmoreland accused me of being a yellow-bellied sonofabitch."

The response throughout the nation was electric. He was hailed by supporters and opponents alike, and his popularity, measured in the polls, rose dramatically.

Within a few days, the word came that Hanoi, too, along with most of America, had been listening. For the first time in the long struggle, the Communists were willing to talk.

The day Hanoi's encouraging response to his speech came in, the President held a reconciling meeting with Robert Kennedy, who had entered the race for the nomination after McCarthy's strong showing in New Hampshire. He met also with Hubert Humphrey, who would soon join that race. It was a tranquil and healing day, the last to be seen for a long time.

On April 4, Martin Luther King was assassinated in Memphis, and overnight the world was a different place.

There was a cruel irony in the fact that his death, after a lifetime of devotion to nonviolence, set off a wave of rioting that for a week swept through more than a hundred American cities. In the nation's capital, arson and pillaging blackened city blocks less than a mile from the White House. Privately, the President, in shock and dismay, "wondered what we were coming to." Publicly he moved to restore order. He sent Federal troops where they were needed and requested. He enlisted the aid of black leaders in calming the rioters. But he also saw a chance to wrest—as he had before—something of substance from the chaos: he proposed, and within a week Congress passed, a new civil rights bill banning discrimination in the sale or renting of housing. Somewhat to his own surprise, this would be only one of 56 bills, including important consumer protection and conservation measures, he managed to get passed during the year despite his lame-duck status. But the legislative victories, satisfying as they were, were scant buffer against the tragedies.

Scarcely had the nation had time to recover from the turmoil of King's death than it was plunged again into nightmare with the assassination of Robert Kennedy in Los Angeles. In his campaign, Kennedy had shown himself to be a vibrant leader, displaying much the same kind of charismatic magnetism his brother had shown eight years before, gathering about him an excited and devoted constituency, presenting a symbol of freshness and, in many minds, hope. His death, at the hands of a deranged Jordanian, submerged the nation in a confusion of emotions: grief, disbelief, even fear. "What is happening to our country?" the majority leader of the Senate, Mike Mansfield, asked the First

**A stunned Johnson family watches the televised scenes of violence in the streets of Chicago at the Democratic convention, which nominates Hubert Humphrey for President.**

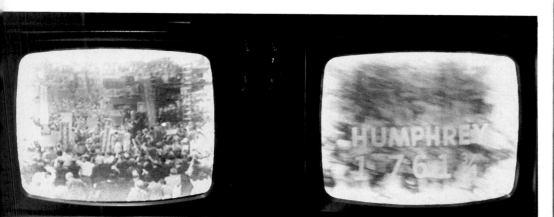

The President's action on March 31—
halting bombing over most of North Vietnam—
led to talks with the North Vietnamese
in Paris. But those talks bog down, and
the President is considering the suspension
of all bombing. In what he would later
remember as "a blur of meetings and
phone calls, of cables and conferences,"
Johnson discusses all possibilities
with his advisers and members of Congress.
His chief concern is that an end to all
bombing might pose a danger to U.S. troops.

Lady. "All day long," she said, "I heard this cacophony over and over—What is our country coming to? What is happening to us? Are we a sick society?"

The President endeavored to give the American people his own answers to those questions. "Two hundred million Americans did not strike down Robert Kennedy," he said in an address to the nation, "any more than they struck down President John Kennedy…or Dr. Martin Luther King…It would be wrong…to conclude from this act that our country itself is sick, that it has lost its balance, its sense of direction, even its common decency."

But the questions would linger, casting their shadow over the entire year.

Johnson had used his famed powers of persuasion to get Abe Fortas to accept a seat on the Supreme Court in 1965—and in doing so, he ruefully said later, "I ruined his life." The "ruin" he referred to began in mid-1968 when Earl Warren announced his retirement and the President nominated Fortas to take his place as Chief Justice. Fortas, he said, was "as good, fine, patriotic and concerned a human as I ever knew. He was liberal and able and courageous, and would do what's good for the people." He thought he had the votes before Fortas's nomination—and that of Federal Judge Homer Thornberry to replace him—went forward. But the opposition was too strong. The nominal objection was that Fortas had counseled the President while he was a member of the Court—"a straw man, pure and simple," Johnson maintained. "Our history is filled with examples of Supreme Court Justices who not only advised Presidents but carried out political chores for them." The real reason he ascribed to Fortas's being "too progressive for the Republicans and the Southern conservatives in the Senate" who were counting on Richard Nixon becoming the next President and giving them a Chief Justice "more to their liking." After two months of

**W**hen I left for Vietnam, the President gave me a small battery-operated tape recorder and several blank tapes so that I could send Lynda occasional recordings and could play back tapes she sent me.

Normally, I would record my tapes when we got back to a combat base after an operation. Because of the heat, the batteries would become weak, so that when the tapes were played on a machine with fresh batteries, the message would be speeded up and the pitch of the voices increased to the point where it was difficult to hear what was being said.

On one of Lynda's return tapes she told me her father had said that he couldn't understand how she "had married someone who didn't have enough sense to use fresh batteries." My initial response was not unlike Bill Moyers's comeback when the President told him that he couldn't hear the grace Bill was delivering over dinner one night: "Mr. President, I wasn't speaking to you."

Most of the tapes Lynda and I exchanged had a lot of the talk you might expect from a recently married couple. I can only trust that the tapes her father found of particular interest were ones in which I described the operations we had participated in. If so, I think they gave him some of the texture of the war at company levels—without all of the gory details.

—CHARLES S. ROBB

**Three months before
the end of the Administration,
a new member
joins the family: Lucinda Robb.**

**Alone in the Cabinet Room,
the President listens
to an account of
action in Vietnam
from his son-in-law,
Marine Captain Charles Robb.**

humiliation, Fortas asked that his name be withdrawn, and Johnson complied. The following year, Fortas would resign from the Court altogether when it was disclosed that as a Justice he had accepted retainers from a private client.

Midway through the year, Johnson finally got Congress to approve the surtax he had tried to get in 1967 to pay the rising cost of the war. But it came at a steep price. Before the committee with responsibility for fiscal matters would send it forward for a vote, it demanded a quid-pro-quo reduction in expenditures of $6 billion. It was a bitter pill for the President, this hard evidence of the war's intrusion into the Great Society. Some members of his Cabinet advised him not to give in. "They wanted me to tell the Congress to go to hell," he remembered, "and I understood them." But the alternative he saw—a devastating inflation— would be worse. He took the occasion to recount an experience from his early days in Congress when he was trying to get electric power for the farmers in his district. Angered at the recalcitrance of utility company executives, he broke up a meeting by telling one of them that he could "go to hell." "I felt relieved,"

**Although convinced now that all bombing should be halted, and assured that it will not endanger American soldiers, the President is prevented from taking this final action because the South Vietnamese suddenly refuse to cooperate. But finally the way is clear, and the bombers are grounded.**

he said, and the farmers "loved it." But an older man, his mentor and supporter Alvin Wirtz, whose influence had a life-long effect on Johnson, brought him down to earth by observing that his outburst "left us back where we started. The power companies still owned the power lines and the farmers still needed electricity." "You can *tell* a man to go to hell," Wirtz told the young LBJ, "but you can't *make* him go." Johnson found that lesson "particularly apt," he said, in the impasse over the surtax. He could tell the Congress to go to hell, but he wouldn't get the tax, and the country would suffer. As it developed, with the surtax in hand he was able to submit to the Congress a balanced budget before he left the White House.

He had planned to cap his last year with a trip to the Soviet Union to discuss with Chairman Kosygin the limitation and reduction of strategic weapons. The news was scheduled to be released on August 21. But on August 20, word came

mphrey

The Evening Star

Bombing of N. Vietnam Halts

Johnson Says Plan
Is Not Foolproof

**D**id we legislate too much? Perhaps. Did we stub our toes? Of course. We made mistakes, plenty of them. Often, we did not recognize that government could not do it all. And, of course, there were overpromises.

But our excesses were based on high hopes and great expectations and were fueled by the frustration of seeing so much poverty and ignorance and illness amidst such wealth. We simply could not accept poverty, ignorance, and hunger as intractable, permanent features of American society. There was no child we could not feed; no adult we would not put to work; no disease we could not cure; no toy, food, or appliance we could not make safer; no air or water we could not clean. It was all part of asking, "not how much, but how good; not only how to create wealth, but how to use it; not only how fast we [were] going, but where we [were] headed."

—Joseph A. Califano

to the White House of the impending Soviet incursion into Czechoslovakia to stem the growing demands there for more freedom. The summit meeting was off. The stream of disappointments remained unbroken.

Nor would it change when the Democrats met in convention in Chicago to nominate their candidate to succeed him. Johnson stayed at his ranch in Texas, but he saw on television, as the world did, the ugly confrontations between delegations inside the convention hall, and between the young and the police in the streets and parks. In 1968, the Democratic party was one of the walking wounded from the Vietnam battlefield. The President telephoned Hubert Humphrey to offer his congratulations after Humphrey secured the nomination, but they both knew it was a damaged prize.

Johnson's campaign for Humphrey was not as active as some thought it should be, "because," he said, "I had promised the nation in my speech of March 31 that I would keep the Presidency out of politics, and because that obviously was what the Humphrey organization preferred." He accepted the latter reason philosophically. The surge in popularity he had enjoyed after his withdrawal from the political scene had been brief. As the war ground on, the internal hostilities resumed, and he understood that the Vice President "had the mounting dissatisfaction toward me and our Administration going against him." His efforts were nonetheless effective, at least with some. After one televised speech, the Smothers Brothers, whose TV comedy program had taken a number of potshots at him, wrote that they were "quite moved." Because of "our emotional feelings regarding the war," they said, "we frequently disregarded the many good works and the progress the country has made under your administration." (Johnson responded that criticism was "the price of leadership." He returned their compliment by saying, "You have given the gift of laughter.")

*In 1966, our love affair with the Texas hill country led to our building our own ranch house some 40 miles from the LBJ Ranch. In this house we saw the New Year in with the President and Lady Bird and friends in 1966 and again in 1968. This photograph was taken on New Year's Eve 1968 as the President looked forward to shedding the burdens of office three weeks later. We cannot recall what we were all singing, but the photograph speaks for itself of the camaraderie we all enjoyed as we awaited the new year— possibly also of why the President took so many precautions so that he could have these informal moments with family and friends away from the glare of the press.*

—MATHILDE AND ARTHUR KRIM

**The President's staff during the final week:** (seated, left to right) **Joseph Califano and Walt Rostow** (standing, first row) **Mike Manatos, James Jones, and Ernest Goldstein** (standing, second row) **Barefoot Sanders, Larry Temple, President Johnson, De Vier Pierson, and Charles Murphy** (standing, third row) **Robert Hardesty, Tom Johnson, Harry Middleton, George Christian, Harry McPherson, Lawrence Levinson, and William Hopkins.**

**F**or the sixth and the last time, I present to the Congress my assessment of the state of the Union…

Every President lives, not only with what is, but with what has been and what could be…

Although the struggle for progressive change is continuous, there are times when a watershed is reached, when there is if not really a break with the past, at least the fulfillment of many of its oldest hopes, and a stepping forth into a new environment, to seek new goals.

I think the past five years have been such a time…

Now, my friends in Congress, I want to conclude with a few very personal words to you…

Most all of my life as a public official has been spent here in this building. For 38 years…

*I have known these halls, and I have known most of the men pretty well who walked them.*

*I know the questions that you face. I know the conflicts that you endure. I know the ideals that you seek to serve...*

*Now, it is time to leave. I hope it may be said, a hundred years from now, that by working together we helped to make our country more just, more just for all of its people, as well as to ensure and guarantee the blessings of liberty for all of our posterity.*

*That is what I hope. But I believe that at least it will be said that we tried.*

Final Address to the Congress on the State of the Union
January 14, 1969

"The golden coin is almost spent,"
Lady Bird records in her diary.
There is a moment of reflection,
a welcome to the new Chief Executive,
and a Presidency ends.

One final decision remained: whether to stop *all* the bombing of targets in North Vietnam. Since March 31, bombs had been dropped only in the area close to the zone separating the two Vietnams, where the enemy buildup was a direct threat to American forces. As summer moved into fall, the Administration debated the consequences of a total cessation—whether it would actually expose the troops to increased danger; whether it would revive the talks with the North Vietnamese, which had started in Paris and then stalled; what the political implications would be domestically: would it help Humphrey? or create a backlash? would the Republicans cry foul? After weeks of torturing the issue, Johnson was ready to gamble that the risk was worth taking. But then the South Vietnamese leaders, whose concurrence he wanted, dragged their feet, having been advised by the Republicans to wait until after the election. Finally, on October 31, the word: we'll do it anyway.

Eleven days later, Nixon won the election. What influence the bombing decision had on the voting, one way or the other, would never be known. But the talks in Paris resumed.

At Christmastime, three astronauts, the crew of Apollo 8, flew in orbit around the moon, just a few miles above its surface. More thrilling experiences would come later in America's space adventure, but it was still a luminous moment. It was one of the few such moments in Johnson's final year as President.

January, the last month, was better, "the windup time," Lady Bird called it. It was a season of farewells: to Cabinet and staff, to the press and the Congress. Johnson went to Capitol Hill to deliver his final State of the Union Message, the first outgoing President since John Adams to do so. He decided on this course, he told the legislators, out of "pure sentiment," because of his long ties with the institution. They responded in kind. They received him warmly, stood to cheer him, and sang "Auld Lang Syne" as he left the chamber and the tumultuous years behind him.

# EPILOGUE

Lyndon Johnson lived for four years and two days after he left the White House. If he missed the arena of action in which he had moved for four decades, he never showed it. Accounts of his being "bored," "bitter," "resentful," or "frustrated" in his retirement contradict the recollections of his family and those who were close to him. Lady Bird called this time the "milk and honey years," when he was relaxed and mellow and, albeit on a smaller stage, fulfilled.

He became a full-time rancher, endlessly crossing his land to inspect cattle and fences and salt licks, supervising the laying of irrigation pipe, never tiring of the pageant of deer leaping at dusk over his pastures.

He did not abandon the past; he was fiercely protective of it. He wanted his memoirs, *The Vantage Point*, to be a full account of his Presidency. Those of us who worked with him on the book would discuss the contents with him before drafting the chapters, as we had done with his speeches in the White House, and then turn the product over to him for his review and editing. We experienced considerable frustration in the process: the preliminary talks were usually delightful—LBJ at his storytelling best, often relating affairs of state as if they had happened in Johnson City. But transferring these reminiscences to paper rarely survived his final review. Such informality, he felt, was somehow demeaning to the office. So the prose became less vivid and more stately, and we watched helplessly as Lyndon Johnson disappeared behind it.

Particularly with Vietnam did he want the record complete, every meeting and memorandum, the documentation for every action included, as if from this massive compilation the final truth of that agonizing adventure would be revealed for all to see and finally understand. Vietnam continued to torment him. His inability to end the war—"with honor"—was his most bitter disappointment. "Man can" had always been his expression of an activist political philosophy. In the last years of his life he amended it: "Man can do anything he sets his mind to do, except find a way out of the Vietnam war."

There was a decided ambivalence in his reflections on the war. To some— Walt Rostow, who had succeeded Bundy as National Security Adviser, and Jim Cross, who had been his pilot and senior military aide—he expressed the wish that he had taken stronger action and gone for a military victory. Leonard

The Presidential library housing
Johnson's papers and the record
of his 40 years in public life
is the scene of his last triumphs.

Marks, his USIA director, related a conversation in which Johnson seemed to regret he had not simply declared his objectives achieved in Vietnam and brought the troops home, as Senator George Aiken had once proposed. With others—Tom Johnson, Bob Hardesty, and myself—he endlessly probed all the alternatives, exploring the "what ifs," always coming back to the conviction that he could have taken no other course, sure that history would agree, but constantly haunted by the cost paid in death and suffering and divisiveness.

He did not live to see American troops withdrawn from Vietnam, or the subsequent collapse of the South Vietnamese forces, or the enemy's triumphant entry into Saigon, or the U.S. helicopters lifting for the last time from the roof of the American Embassy—the final ignominious image in the long adventure. But, on the other hand, neither did he live to hear the judgment of some Pacific leaders—notably Lee Kuan Yew, Prime Minister of Singapore, and Michael Cook, Australian Ambassador to the United States—that, despite the final defeat, America's stand in Vietnam had bought sufficient time for the new countries of Asia, emerging from their colonial past, to build their nations free of domination by other powers.

He knew that his political opposition would try to scuttle his Great Society, but he did not think they would succeed. His view of history was both cyclical and progressive. He believed that what had been achieved in his time, even if some of the programs were set back for a while, would eventually be expanded and built upon, as he had built upon the accomplishments of Roosevelt and Truman.

The library that houses Johnson's papers is on the campus of the University of Texas in Austin. Construction began in 1968 and was completed in May 1971, when the building was dedicated. Like all Presidential libraries, its chief purpose is to maintain and make available for historical study the voluminous records that document his career. Like others also, there is a museum that portrays for the general public the highlights of the Johnson years.

Johnson took a personal interest in the progress of the building's construction. He was not particularly involved in the museum area until the final weeks. Then, after walking through the space one day and examining the exhibits being installed, he complained that there was not enough about the controversies of the period. "I don't want another damn credibility gap," he said. So barely a month before the library was to open, a new exhibition was created, showing the furors that had rocked his Administration, mainly over Vietnam, but also attending the passage of Medicare and Federal aid to education and some of the other programs hotly disputed in their day.

He wanted something else in that exhibit as well. "I received some pretty mean mail," he said. "Let's put the meanest letter I ever got in there." The archivists went on an extensive search through the millions of pieces of correspondence in the files. Nothing they turned up satisfied Johnson, who now looked on the exhibit as his own creation. One afternoon he took a hand in the search himself, going through box after box, steeped in the rancor that once had hounded him. Finally, with a flourish of triumph, he produced a postcard written by a man in Linden, California. It read: "I demand that you, as a gutless sonofabitch, resign as President of the United States." "You can't get much meaner than that," Johnson decided. The postcard went into the exhibition.

The library's first major project, about a year after its dedication, was to open the papers relating to education, and commemorate the event with a symposium in which leaders in the field would discuss further initiatives the government might take. Johnson was intensely interested in the symposium. I met with him at the ranch frequently and talked almost daily to him on the phone about the plans. In the meantime the archivists were reviewing the papers. Those that were questionable came to me for resolution; most of them stayed stacked on my desk without being resolved.

About ten days before the occasion, Johnson called, and this time he wanted to talk not about the conference but about the papers. "We're opening everything that has anything to do with education, aren't we?" he asked.

"Well, all that *can* be opened," I answered.

"Now, what does that mean?" he demanded.

I reminded him that the deed of gift he signed when he turned the papers over to the Government, following usual procedure, stipulated that papers that would be injurious or embarrassing to living persons should be kept closed for a while.

He pretended not to understand what I was saying—a not-untypical Johnson ploy. "Give me an example," he said.

I had a desktop full of such examples, and I picked one. It was a memorandum from Joe Califano to the President with a rather scurrilous reference to Congresswoman Edith Green. There was a silence. Then Johnson said: "Edith's heard worse things than that. Who else is that memo going to hurt?"

I pointed out that Califano, then Democratic party counsel, was having to work with a lot of people from different camps, and might be troubled by it.

"When you were appointed director of the library," Johnson said, "was there anything in your job description that said you were supposed to hold the Democratic party together?" He asked for other examples, and I gave him several. He disposed of all of them in much the same fashion. Then he asked: "Are you going to try to treat me the same way?"

I said, choosing my way carefully, that he deserved the same consideration anyone else did, and if—but he interrupted. "Good men have been trying to save my reputation for 40 years," he said, "and not a damn one's succeeded. What makes you think you can?" Another silence. Then: "I suppose you think that if I pick up the paper one day and read about something in these files I don't like, I'll raise hell."

"Mr. President," I acknowledged, "that thought has occurred to me."

"Well, if that ever happens," he said, "here's what I want you to do. I want you to go out and sit on the hill in front of the library. Take a lot of deep breaths, and think of everything we've been through to get this library opened. And then you come back to your office and you call me. I'll be right here waiting for your call because I'll be expecting it. You say, 'Mr. President'—because that's the way you talk, you're always very polite—'one of us is full of shit and we've got to decide right now who it is.'"

The library has a reputation of being liberal in its policy of opening papers. The policy stems from that day.

The symposium was a success. Johnson used the occasion to articulate once more his own philosophy of government in the United States, the concept that had undergirded the Great Society and survived undamaged through all the political wars. "This country," he said, "has the money to do anything it has the guts to do and the will to do and the vision to do." He was the education President again, speaking to educators. They responded to him as one of their own and gave him the kind of ovation that once had been his daily fare.

Less than a year later there was another symposium, this one on civil rights. Many of the old giants of the movement were there—Clarence Mitchell, Roy Wilkins, Vernon Jordan, Hubert Humphrey, Earl Warren—and some of the new ones as well: Barbara Jordan, Yvonne Burke. Julian Bond, then a state legislator in Georgia, who had marched in the streets against Johnson to protest the Vietnam war, took to the podium to praise him: "When the forces demanded and the mood permitted, for once an activist, human-hearted man had his hand on the levers of power and a vision beyond the next election. He was there when we and the nation needed him, and, oh by God, do I wish he was there now."

These were Lyndon Johnson's last days. He had come through two heart attacks; in another month a third would take him off. He had been quietly putting his affairs in order. It was almost as if he knew this appearance would be

The old schoolteacher returns to the classroom. On occasions that the students find memorable, LBJ shares his concept of government with undergraduates at his alma mater, Southwest Texas State University, and (overleaf) with men and women at the School of Public Affairs, which bears his name, at the University of Texas in Austin.

The President is buried in the family graveyard, under a giant oak down the road from the ranch, on the banks of the Pedernales.

The final years were "the good quiet years," Lady Bird would say when he was gone. "He found his pleasure in being a rancher and a grandfather and a neighbor."

his last. But of all the causes, this was the one on which he had hoped to stake his claim in history; so against his doctors' orders he had come. He went further than he ever had before in calling for special treatment to redress old injustices. He pledged the constant support of his failing heart and the proceeds from the sale of "a few wormy cows" to the cause that bound them together. He ended with the words of their own movement—"We shall overcome"—that had so stirred them when he made the words ring before the Congress. Their cheers and their company revived him, and for a while he was again on the courthouse steps, telling the old stories, preaching the old progressive gospel, surrounded by people who believed in him.

He did not talk about death much, but it was on his mind. He attended the memorial service of a friend. It was held in a Catholic cathedral, and although he had shown a decided interest in Catholicism, it did not extend to that institution's ceremonial pomp. The cathedral had been close and stuffy, the odor of incense cloying. The mourners had been celebrated figures.

It prompted him to make his wishes clear: "When I die," he told Lady Bird in the company of other guests, "I don't just want our friends who can come in their private planes. I want the men in their pickup trucks and the women whose slips hang down below their dresses to be welcome, too."

When he was buried in the family graveyard along the Pedernales on a cold January afternoon ten days later, they were all there, the men who landed their planes on the runway and the neighbors from the ranches and towns around who brought their families by truck.

Before he was buried, his body lay in the library in Austin and in the Rotunda of the Capitol in Washington. Lady Bird and the daughters with their husbands stood by the casket in both places to greet the thousands who shuffled past, his supporters and detractors alike.

Although it was 1973, the Sixties had not yet been played out, and many of the young in the long lines had marched against him in the streets. Lady Bird remembered "one young man, very bearded, who stood before me so stoically and bowed slightly." "My apologies," he said to her.

"It's all right," she told him. "He wanted to change things, too."

# BIBLIOGRAPHY

The following works have been cited in the text or were consulted in its preparation.

PRINTED MATERIAL

Berman, Larry. *Lyndon Johnson's War*. New York: 1989.
Bornet, Vaughn Davis. *The Presidency of Lyndon B. Johnson*.
 Lawrence, Kansas: 1983.
Bundy, William P. Unpublished manuscript on deposit at the Lyndon B. Johnson Library,
 Austin, Texas.
Caroli, Betty Boyd. *First Ladies*. New York: 1987.
Caute, David. *The Year of the Barricades: A Journey Through 1968*. New York: 1987.
Christian, George. *The President Steps Down*. New York: 1970.
Divine, Robert. *Exploring the Johnson Years*. Austin, Texas: 1981.
_____ *The Johnson Years*. Vol. II. Lawrence, Kansas: 1987.
Evans, Rowland and Robert Novak. *Lyndon B. Johnson: The Exercise of Power*.
 New York: 1966.
Firestone, Bernard J. and Robert C. Vogt, eds. *Lyndon Baines Johnson and the Uses of
 Power*. Westport, Connecticut: 1988.
Gould, Lewis L. *Lady Bird Johnson and the Environment*. Lawrence, Kansas: 1988.
Hardesty, Robert L. *The LBJ the Nation Seldom Saw*. San Marcos, Texas: 1983.
Herring, George C. *America's Longest War*. New York: 1979.
Isaacson, Walter and Evan Thomas. *The Wise Men*. New York: 1986.
Johnson, Lady Bird. *White House Diary*. New York: 1970.
Johnson, Lyndon B. *Public Papers of the Presidents*. Washington, D.C.: 1965, 1966, 1967,
 1968, 1970.
_____ *The Vantage Point: Perspectives of the Presidency, 1963-1969*.
 New York: 1971.
Jordan, Barbara C. and Elspeth D. Rostow, eds. *The Great Society: A Twenty-Year Critique*.
 Austin, Texas: 1986.
Karnow, Stanley. *Vietnam: A History*. New York: 1983.
Kearns, Doris. *Lyndon Johnson and the American Dream*. New York: 1976.
Keylin, Arleen and Laurie Barnett, eds. *The Sixties as Reported by "The New York Times."*
 New York: 1980.
Livingston, William S., Lawrence C. Dodd, and Richard L. Schott, eds. *The Presidency and
 the Congress*. Austin, Texas: 1979.
MacNeil, Robert, ed. *The Way We Were: 1963, The Year Kennedy Was Shot*. New York: 1988.
McPherson, Harry. *A Political Education*. Boston: 1972.
Meyerson, Joel D. *Images of a Lengthy War*. Washington, D.C.: 1986.
Miller, Merle. *Lyndon*. New York: 1980.
Reedy, George. *Lyndon B. Johnson: A Memoir*. New York: 1982.
Rooney, Robert G., Ed. *Equal Opportunity in the United States*. Austin, Texas: 1973.
Rostow, W. W. *The Diffusion of Power*. New York: 1972.
Schoenbaum, Thomas J. *Waging Peace and War*. New York: 1988.
Sheehan, Neil. *A Bright Shining Lie: John Paul Vann and America in Vietnam*.
 New York: 1988.
Smith, Nancy Kegan and Mary C. Ryan, eds. *Modern First Ladies*. Washington, D.C.: 1989.
Tolo, Kenneth, ed. *Educating a Nation*. Austin, Texas: 1973.
U.S. Congress. Senate. Committee on Foreign Relations. *The U.S. Government and the
 Vietnam War*. Parts I, II, III. Report prepared by the Congressional Research Service,
 Library of Congress. 98th Congress.
Valenti, Jack. *A Very Human President*. New York: 1975.


FILMS ON DEPOSIT AT THE LYNDON B. JOHNSON LIBRARY, AUSTIN, TEXAS

*The First Lady: A Portrait of Lady Bird Johnson*. Guggenheim Productions, Inc.
*The Great Society Remembered*. Guggenheim Productions, Inc.
*Interview with Lady Bird Johnson*
*Lyndon B. Johnson*
*The Johnson Style*. Guggenheim Productions, Inc.

# INDEX

Page numbers in *italics* refer to photographs and captions.

# PHOTOGRAPH CREDITS

Unless noted below, the photographs in this book were taken by YOICHI OKAMOTO and are the property of the Lyndon B. Johnson Library, Austin, Texas.

Numbers refer to pages.

MIKE GEISSINGER: 64 (bottom), 65 (right), 68 (middle and bottom left), 70-71, 182 (both photos), 183 (bottom left), 193 (top and bottom right), 194 (right), 200, 202 (lower left), 228 (top), 229, 234, 249, 254-55; JACK KIGHTLINGER: 211 (middle), 246, 252; ROBERT KNUDSEN: 98, 142-43, 158-59, 159 (lower left and right), 172-73, 176-77, 207 (right), 210, 211 (top), 212 (all photos), 213 (top and bottom), 214, 215 (top), 218, 247; O. J. RAPP: 47 (bottom left), 54 (top), 68 (middle right); KEVIN SMITH: 161 (middle right), 217; DONALD STODERL: 47 (bottom right), 54 (bottom); CECIL STOUGHTON: 10-11, 27, 28, 29 (top), 30, 31, 35, 36-37, 38, 39, 40-41, 42, 44-45, 46 (all photos), 47 (top), 48-49, 50-51, 52, 55, 56-57, 77 (both photos), 83 (bottom), 97 (bottom); FRANK WOLFE: 32-33, 65 (left), 66 (top right), 76, 135 (right), 142 (middle left), 143 (middle right), 154-55, 179, 207 (top and middle), 211 (bottom), 213 (middle), 220, 221, 229, 256, and Epilogue; UNIDENTIFIED: 53, 72, 96 (middle left), 208, 209, 215 (middle, middle right, bottom), 235.

The following photographs were taken by ABBIE ROWE and are the property of the National Archives of the United States, Washington, D.C.: 13, 34, 74, 86, 99, 105 (bottom).

The following photographs were taken for the UPI and are the property of The Bettmann Archive, New York City: 109 (bottom right), 117.

The photograph at the top of page 83 was taken by CHARLES GORRY.